RIVER TO RIM

A GUIDE TO PLACE NAMES

ALONG THE COLORADO RIVER

IN GRAND CANYON

FROM LAKE POWELL TO LAKE MEAD

By Nancy Brian

EARTHQUEST PRESS, FLAGSTAFF

1992

Library of Congress Catalog Card Number: 92-90263
ISBN 1-881438-00-7

First Edition
Earthquest Press, Flagstaff, Arizona
Manufactured in the United States of America

Printed by Northland Printing
Flagstaff, Arizona
Times Roman Type

Cover photograph titled, "Grand Canyon of the Colorado," by William Henry Jackston, circa 1883, No. 1069, W.H. Jackson Photo. & Pub. Co., Denver, Colorado, Photographers of Rocky Mountain Scenery.

All photographs reproduced in this edition courtesy of Russell Books & Bindery, private collection, Spokane, Washington.

CONTENTS

ACKNOWLEDGMENTS

Many people helped in the completion of this work and I owe thanks to all of them.

My appreciation and thanks go the following individuals who gave of their knowledge and time: Bill Breed, Barbara Brewer, Gene Buell, Christopher Coder, Mike Castelli, Kim Crumbo, Mike Ebersole, Dave Foster, Dottie House, C. David Hellyer, Dart Judd, Martin Litton, Kent Morby, Paul Martin, La Van Martineau, John O'Brien, John Rote, George C. "Black George" Simmons, Hal G. Stephens, Scott Thybony, and Henry W. Toll, Jr., and Tom Workman.

I would like to gratefully acknowledge my reviewers for their suggestions and assistance: Jan Balsom, George Billingsley, Harvey Butchart, Annie Russell, Richard Quartaroli, and Peter Winn. Their knowledge helped to make this book more accurate and informative. Sandy Thybony provided many helpful editing comments. I claim full responsibility for any shortcomings which may remain.

I would like to thank the staff of Northern Arizona University's Cline Special Collections Library, the Arizona Historical Society's Southern Division, the Museum of Northern Arizona, and the John Wesley Powell Museum for their assistance. Roger Payne, the Executive Secretary of the Domestic Names Committee for the U.S. Board on Geographic Names, was especially helpful.

Special thanks go to my husband Terry for his support and humor and to my sister Annie Russell for her encouragement, enthusiasm, and preparation of the maps and geologic cross section.

FORWARD

Thirteen year old Patricia, who was on our raft floating through the Grand Canyon, looked at me and wailed, "Doesn't anybody get out of here alive?"

Three days earlier, we had left Lee's Ferry on a commercial raft trip. Between rapids, while my husband Terry motored downstream, I would tell our 14 passengers about the rock layers, flowering cacti, names of side canyons, birds, and bits of Colorado River history.

Vivid in Patricia's memory were only the gory details of navigational disasters: the old ferry boat tipping over and drowning passengers at Lee's Ferry, F.M. Brown's untimely boat flip and drowning below Soap Creek Rapid in 1889, and the subsequent inscription of this event etched by Peter Hansbrough who, along with Henry Richards, died only six days later at 25 Mile Rapid.

Patricia's question came after I pointed out Chuar Butte opposite the Little Colorado River. Here, two commercial airplanes had collided. It was then that I realized that a fair number of the stories had literally ended in the Grand Canyon. I laughed and reassured her that we were safe and we had never lost anyone in over 120 trips through the Grand Canyon. But, her question really started me thinking.

Places along the Colorado River have always been fixed in my mind with stories, facts, and memories. I am a taxonomist by nature and ultimately by education. I like names for plants, rocks, and places. With names, they become old friends. I used to consult guides to place names and would get frustrated when a place was not listed and the mystery solved. I wanted to know more and began to search through a century of literature. Bit by bit, the secrets were unraveled and this book started to write itself.

A friend told me that there were two things to writing: starting and stopping. He was right. There are place names that I haven't been able to decipher. If you know another meaning or a place that should be listed, write to me at Earthquest Press and I will update this guide. But for now, for your enjoyment and knowledge, here is the extended self-guided tour to places along the Colorado River in Grand Canyon. Happy Trails Amigos.

"From Bissel's Point, Canon of the Colorado," No. 6486B, W.H. Jackson Photo. & Pub. Co., Denver, Colo. Note: This photograph not taken at Bissel Point (Comanche Point) but at a point west of Lipan Point.

INTRODUCTION

What is in a name? Does it really describe a place? Perhaps Irvin Cobb was right when he said in 1913, "It is generally conceded that the Grand Canyon of Arizona beggars description...you take one look -- and instantly you lose all your former standards of comparison. You stand there gazing down the raw, red gullet of that great gosh-awful gorge, and you feel your self-importance shriveling up to nothing inside of you. You haven't an adjective left to your back." (15) Happily, we can dispense with names whenever we want and just enjoy the canyon.

However, a name does identify a place and gives us a point of reference. It is human nature to name things. The human brain has isolated cortical areas which deal specifically with naming. It would seem that we cannot tolerate a prominent place without a name. Place names help us to perceive the world around us and personalize the landscape. Some may feel that a name robs the landscape of its character by reducing it to human terms. But, outlandish or weird names help us to grasp the overwhelming nature of the Grand Canyon of the Colorado River. Wallace Stegner queeried, "Still, what should one do for names in a geological funhouse?" (155)

George Gaylord Simpson, an eminent vertebrate paleontologist, summed it all up when he wrote, "The passion for naming things is an odd human trait. It is strange that men always feel so much more at ease when they have put appellations on the things around them and that a wild, new region almost seems familiar and subdued once enough names have been used on it, even though in fact it is not changed in the slightest. Or, on second thought, it is perhaps not really strange. The urge to name must be as old as the human race, as old as speech which is one of the really fundamental characteristics by which we rise above the brutes, and thus a basic and essential part of the human spirit or soul. The naming fallacy is common enough even in science. Many a scientist claims to have explained some phenomenon, when in truth all he has done is to give it a name." (93)

This guide is an expansion of *Grand Canyon Place Names* which has served for many years and from which some of this guide is drawn. Information is referenced by number, but it is hoped that the stories behind the names will lead you to read the original sources to find out the "rest of the story." A bibliographic listing of references is included as a springboard to further reading, but it is by no means complete or all encompassing.

THE HISTORY OF PLACE NAMES IN GRAND CANYON

The history of Grand Canyon is chronicled with place names that reflect the stories and perceptions of the people who have explored, surveyed, and lived from the Canyon's floor to its rim. The Spanish conquistadores and friars were the first (after the Native peoples) to bestow names fifty years after Columbus arrived in the New World. But it remained until maps were made for place names to be used consistently.

John Wesley Powell endowed the canyon with many romantic and descriptive names during and after his two expeditions in the late 1800s. He adopted many Indian words and named some of the rock layers and cliffs after colors. Several years later, Clarence E. Dutton, in describing the history of the Tertiary age rocks, gave them oriental and religious names. He was fond of architectural metaphor and pinnacles, buttes, and monuments became temples, shrines, thrones, and castles.

This fanciful legacy of heroic nomenclature was carried on from 1903 to 1923 by Francois E. Matthes and Richard T. Evans. They prepared topographic maps of the region and used mythological, classical, and religious names, including those of the Arthurian legends. The surveyors of the 1923 Birdseye Expedition bestowed mileage names to rapids and tributaries from Lee's Ferry to Pearce Ferry. Pioneers, miners, and stockmen brought family and mineral names into common usage. Finally, the Park Service, hikers, and river runners gave names to points along the rim, arches, rapids, and beaches.

Grand Canyon place names are the language in which the Colorado River country's autobiography is written. Names have gone from the sublime (Point Sublime) to the secular (Randy's Rock). Place names can be descriptive (Great Thumb Mesa), non-descriptive (Turquoise Canyon), personal names (Kolb Arch), transplanted geographic names (Doll's House), commemorative names for a date or an event (Deubendorff Rapids), religious or social names (Tabernacle), casual and whimsical (Tater Canyon), metamorphosed (Stephens Aisle from Esteban), or of mixed type (Temple Butte). Features were often named spontaneously (Sockdolager) or to immortalize famous individuals of the times (President Harding Rapid). Many names are of Native American origin (Hot Na Na) or bestowed by Spanish explorers (Rio Colorado). Names on U.S. Geological Survey (USGS) topographic maps, river guides, or other maps are not always consistent. Many have been altered through time or anglicized. Sinyella now replaces Sinyala, reflecting proper Havasupai spelling. Chuarrumpeak was shortened to Chuar. The Three Castles of the early 1900s was renamed the Sinking Ship in 1930.

U.S. BOARD ON GEOGRAPHIC NAMES

The United States government created the United States Board on Geographic Names (BGN) as an interdepartmental organization in 1890. At that time, President Benjamin Harrison gave it authority to resolve all unsettled questions concerning geographic names. The board's responsibilities were extended in 1906 by President Theodore Roosevelt to include standardization of all geographic names, including name changes and new names. Today, the BGN meets once a month and the foreign names committee once a quarter where decisions are rendered on some 10,000 proposed names or changes. Well over 90 percent of the names submitted are approved. It also develops principles, policies, and procedures governing spelling, use, and application of geographic names for domestic, foreign, Antarctic, and undersea features. Its decisions are legally binding only for the federal government. (79, 108)

The BGN prohibits the use of names which are considered derogatory to any racial, ethnic, or religious group. Also, they consider only names or nicknames of deceased persons. The BGN requires that the person have had some direct association with the feature or have made a significant contribution to the area. Names are given preference which are indigenous to the region, short, euphonious, and in keeping with the character and traditions of the region. (79)

If you are interested in suggesting a place name, submit a written proposal to the BGN (Executive Secretary of Domestic Geographic names, U.S. Board on Geographic Names, USGS, 523 National Center, Reston , VA 22092) and include the following: the full form of the geographic name being proposed, a location and clear identification of the feature (latitude and longitude, if possible), the reason for wishing to name the feature, the origin or meaning of the name, and a basis of knowledge that the feature is unnamed. If you are naming a feature for a person, include their full name, the birth and death dates, and a short biography. Local support for your suggestion is also needed and can be shown by including letters from the appropriate Federal, state, or local administrative authorities or state geographic name authorities; petitions for the name signed by local residents; and newspaper clippings of articles and letters to the editor showing public awareness and endorsement of the proposed name. (79)

Not everyone agrees with place names. In 1906, Francois Matthes protested the naming of features on the Walhalla Plateau. He wrote, "Under the present system we have to memorize *utterly meaningless* Indian words which do not readily associate themselves in the popular mind with the features to which they are applied. Even the best informed among the public must be at a loss to know what they stand for, and there is no dictionary in which they may be looked up. Plain numbers would have done better. Furthermore, the present names are so few and far between that to describe topographic or geologic features, or routes of travel with reference to the few points named requires no end of circumlocution, both tiresome and confusing." (112)

Frederick S. Dellenbaugh, a member of Powell's second expedition in 1871-72, presented another point of view in 1908. He wrote, "It is, in my opinion, a pedantic and ridiculous thing to saddle onto that country a lot of names from European legends like the Arthurian, or the Greek, or Egyptian mythology. Nothing could be more inappropriate to my mind, than 'Holy Grail' Temple in Arizona. I have marked it 'Esperanza' Temple, which seems to me appropriate to the last degree, as the Spaniards were first in the country and their 'hope ran high'...This matter of names worries me greatly, not that I want any romantic or high-sounding names, that I want to avoid the commonplaceness of pedantry." (122)

Controversy continues. In 1976, Otis "Dock" Marston, river historian, wrote to the BGN to contest the naming of Brown's Riffle and Hansbrough-Richards Rapid. He wrote, "These three deaths were due to stupidity and commemoration by place names should be avoided. Continuation of this practice will soon make the course of the Colorado River a memorial to bad navigational practices." (113)

A place name enables us to remember, sort, and differentiate the thousands of places encountered in a lifetime. Place names, especially if they are descriptive or tell of the history of the site, make the recollection meaningful. I hope you will find enough of interest that reading this guide will be well worth your time. May this gazetteer spark your imagination, inform you, and perhaps raise a good argument! Maybe you will someday name a place in the Grand Canyon.

The goal of this guide is to give a history of the place name. It lists points of interest, tributaries, campsites, recent names used by river runners, as well as physiographic terrains, rock formations, and Indian tribes. Approved and colloquial place names are given on a mile-by-mile sequence as the Colorado River flows from Lake Powell to Lake Mead. When possible, information on who named it, when, and why is also included. Spelling follows BGN lists, that found on maps, or in references. Anecdotal information is given to highlight the person or the event and early or other names are listed. A summary of place names by author is given in Appendix A.

Several sources will help you to identify specific features. Visitors and hikers at the canyon rims will find *Grand Canyon Perspectives* (43) very useful for locating places by means of interpretive hand drawn panoramas. Topographic maps will give you a bird's eye view. River runners may find one of the several river guides to the Colorado River helpful.

Places located away from the river are indented under the main drainage. Some points are only visible from the river, while some are only visible from certain points on the rim. Probably a vast majority can only be seen from the air or by hiking. Canyons named after river mile designations are not listed unless there is a story, but a list is given in Appendix B. Names of rapids below River Mile 236 which are now under the waters of Lake Mead are listed as a reminder that these places once existed. If you want to look for a certain place, use the index.

Here is an example of how the guide is organized and what the symbols mean:

RR   RM 35

CANYON CREEK AND RAPIDS: Canyon Creek enters the mainstem Colorado River from river right (RR, as noted on the upper left margin throughout this guide) when viewed downstream. This is a convention used for most rivers. If the creek entered from river left, RL would be in the left margin, while RC means river center. The RM 35 in the upper right margin means that it is located 35 river miles below Lee's Ferry. Negative numbers mean it is located above Lee's Ferry. As a convention, names of rapids are plural. BGN 1908 means that the name was officially approved by the Board on Geographic Names in that year.

5

ITSA BUTTE: Because Itsa Butte is located up the drainage of Canyon Creek, the citation is indented. Apostrophes are excluded from place name headings. A variant name, or one that is a different spelling or word, would be What A Butte. A number in parentheses (83) indicates the reference(s) listed in the bibliography, from which the information was gathered.

"Up Stream fr. Bright Angel Point," No. 1288, Putnam & Valentine, Photo., Los Angeles, Ca.

RM -16 to -170

LAKE POWELL: The lake is named for John Wesley Powell (1834-1902). Powell's parents named him after John Wesley, the founder of the Methodist movement. He began his teaching career in 1852 and fought for the Union in the 20th Illinois Volunteer Infantry. In 1862, he lost his right arm as a result of a severe wound received during the battle of Shiloh. He was discharged in 1865 with the rank of Major and returned to the classroom as professor of geology at Illinois Wesleyan University. He led expeditions into the Colorado Rockies in 1867-68. (54)

Powell is most remembered for his two Colorado River Expeditions. The first departed Green River, Wyoming on May 24, 1869 with nine men and four boats. The journey ended at the mouth of the Virgin River on August 30 with five of the original party and three boats. The second expedition left Green River on May 22, 1871, stopped at Lee's Ferry on October 23, then resumed on August 17, 1872. Departing with two boats and seven men, the trip stopped at Kanab Creek on September 7. Powell reported on his river explorations in 1874 and then published his *Report on the Lands of the Arid Region of the United States* in 1878, which pointed out the difficulties of, and practical solution for, settlement of the western lands. In 1879, he was appointed Director of the newly created Bureau of Ethnology of the Smithsonian Institution and helped to establish the U.S. Geological Survey (USGS). He became the second Director of the USGS in 1881. In 1888, he began the Irrigation Surveys which led to the establishment of the Bureau of Reclamation. (54)

Lake Powell, a reservoir created by Glen Canyon Dam, was first filled in 1980. When full at the 3,700 feet (ft) above sea level elevation, it holds 27 million acre feet, is 186 miles long, and has a shoreline distance of 1,960 miles. Based upon estimates from the Bureau of Reclamation, it is thought to have a "life expectancy" of over 800 years before becoming filled with sediment trapped by the reservoir. The lake is characterized as a "warm" water lake with incomplete circulation, though the upper 230 feet turns over during the autumn. (125)

> **PAGE:** The town of about 7,000 people was named for John Chatfield Page (1887-1955) who spent many years planning and developing upper Colorado River dam sites while serving as Commissioner of Reclamation from 1937 to 1943. (45, 102)

GLEN CANYON: Glen Canyon was named by John Wesley Powell. From his account on August 3, 1869, he wrote, "On the walls, and back many miles into the country, numbers of monument-shaped buttes are observed. So we have a curious ensemble of wonderful features -- carved walls, royal arches, glens, alcove gulches, mounds, and monuments. From which of these features shall we select a name? We decide to call it Glen Canyon." George Bradley, who accompanied Powell's first expedition, states that while on the expedition Powell called the upper half of the canyon (from the Dirty Devil to the San Juan) Mound Canyon and the lower half of the canyon (from the San Juan to Lee's Ferry) Monument Canyon. After 1871, the name Glen Canyon was substituted for the entire reach. (24, 32, 83)

RL/RR   RM -6 to 1
GLEN CANYON NATIONAL RECREATION AREA: Glen Canyon National Recreation area was created in 1972. The National Park Service (NPS), under cooperative agreements with the Bureau of Reclamation in 1958 and 1965, began to acquire land. The NPS manages over one million acres of federal land within the recreation area boundary. The remaining 15 miles of Glen Canyon can be seen between the dam and Lee's Ferry. Here, a blue ribbon trout fishery is managed by the Arizona Game and Fish Department. Trout fingerlings are stocked and a lure-only policy is in effect. Catch and release is suggested by the fishing guides to maintain the quality of the fishery. (54)

RL/RR   RM -16
GLEN CANYON DAM: The dam was authorized in 1956 and the last bucket of concrete was poured in 1963. The turbines and generators were installed between 1963 and 1966. The dam towers 638 ft above the original river channel, has eight generating units, and can produce over 1,350,000 kilowatts of power. Most of this power is sold to hundreds of small and medium sized cities and towns in Arizona, Colorado, Utah, Wyoming, New Mexico, Texas, and Nebraska. The penstocks draw water from 200-230 feet below the surface. The fluctuating flows from the dam are clear and cold (46-54 degrees F) and have severely altered the physical, chemical, and ecological conditions downstream. Flows generally range between 1,000 and 31,500 cubic feet per second (cfs) From 1895-1962, the pre-dam maximum flood was 220,000 cfs, while a flow of about 300,000 cfs is estimated from a 1884 flood mark. On June 29, 1983 a high flow of 97,300 cfs was measured at Lee's Ferry. (12, 105)

In 1969, the Secretary of the Interior and others recommended that the dam's name be changed to Dwight D. Eisenhower Dam as Eisenhower had supported the Colorado River Storage Project, the southwest's gigantic water resource development plan. However, the name was not adopted. (119)

Commercial half to one day float trips depart from the base of the dam for a 15 mile trip to Lee's Ferry where passengers disembark.

> **BEEHIVE:** This is a descriptive name for the dome rock in the Navajo Sandstone resembling a beehive which was partially excavated during construction of the dam and Carl Hayden Visitor's Center.

> **CARL B. HAYDEN VISITOR'S CENTER:** The visitor center at the dam is named after Carl B. Hayden (1877-1972), a senior U.S. Senator from Arizona who served for over fifty years. When Arizona became a state of the Union in February 1912, Hayden was its first representative. He served until retirement in January 1969. A butte in Nankoweap Canyon is named for his father, an Arizona pioneer.

COLORADO RIVER: Southwestern Indians were first to discover the Colorado River and called it by many names which reflect its once turbulent, sediment laden flow. It was known to the Pimas as Buqui Aquimuri (Red River), to the Coco-Maricopas as Gritetho (Great or Grand River), to the Yumas as Javill or Hahweal (Red River), to the Havasupais as Chicamimi Hackatai (Large Canyon with the Roaring Sound), to the Paiutes as Pahaweap (Water Deep Down In The Earth or a Long Way Down To Water) or Pahgaiv (Mighty River), to the Hopis as Pisishbaiyu or Pisisvaiyu (Where Water Flows), and reportedly to the Navajos as Pocketto (Red River) though this may not be a Navajo word. (45, 80, 91, 129)

Europeans also bestowed many names. Francisco de Ulloa is credited with being the first non-Indian to report the river. In 1539, he saw the Colorado River from a ship in the Sea of Cortez (Gulf of California), but gave it no name. (45)

In 1540, Captain Fernando Alarcon was sent by Viceroy Mendoza to take supplies via the Colorado River to meet Francisco Vasquez de Coronado's expedition, which at that time was traveling overland. He called the river El Rio de Buena Guia (The River of Good Guidance), probably as Buena Guia was the motto on Mendoza's coat of arms. (45)

In 1541, Captain Melchior Diaz, one of the two officers sent by Coronado to scout for Captain Fernando Alarcon, traveled overland to the river. He named the river the Rio del Tison (Firebrand River) for the Yuma Indians, who lived along the lower banks of the river. They carried burning brands for the purpose of either relighting camp fires or for mosquito relief. Diaz accidentally speared himself while attempting to spear from horseback a dog that was chasing sheep belonging to the camp. He died 20 days later. (45)

In 1604, Don Juan de Onate, Governor of New Mexico, called the river the Rio Grande de Buena Esperanza (Big River of Good Hope) when he viewed it from near the mouth of the Bill Williams River. Onate was first to use the term Rio Colorado, but in reference to the Little Colorado River's red colored flood waters. (45)

Many years later, Fray Eusebio Francisco Kino called the river the Rio de los Martires (River of the Martyrs). In 1699, his lieutenant, Juan Mateo Manje referred to it as the "true Rio del Norte of the ancients... the fertile Rio Colorado." (45)

In 1774, Fray Francisco Garces, a Franciscan padre, was the first to refer consistently to the river as Rio Colorado in his writings. He noted that the springtime river, when draining the melting snows from the red sandstone country, was tinged with red. Colorado is a Spanish word meaning red colored. Garces was the first European visitor to the Havasupai Indians and traveled along the South Rim. He also noted that the Kaibab Plateau was "a great Sierra." (45)

Fray Francisco Silvestre Velez de Escalante called the Colorado River the Rio Mysterioso (River of Mystery) and occasionally the Rio del Cosnina, in reference to the Havasuapi Indians who lived south of the river. He recognized the Colorado at a point as far north as the Grand and the Gunnison Rivers to be the same as Melchior Diaz's Rio Tison. (45)

In the 1830s, James Ohio Pattie, a famous fur trader, called it the Red River. In the mid-1800s, maps of the region called it variously Rio Colorado del California, Rio Colorado del Poniente, and Rio Colorado del Oriente. In the 1870s, Major John Wesley Powell is credited with the first consistent use of the term Colorado River. (45)

The two branches of the Colorado River are the Green River (longer of the two and originating in Wyoming) and the Grand River (which has its source in Colorado). The people of Colorado wanted the state to have the river it was named for at least partly in its borders, so in 1921, Congress changed the name of the Grand River to the Colorado River. (4, 45)

RR   RM -14
ROPES TRAIL: This descriptive name originates from ropes which used to be attached to the Navajo Sandstone walls and used by residents and Glen Canyon Dam builders to descend into the canyon. The ropes are no longer in place but the trail is still used by hikers.

RL   RM -13
HONEY DRAW: This euphemistic or tongue-in-cheek term refers to the overflow from the sewage treatment ponds located on the rim which used to empty into this draw prior to 1958. The sewage treatment plant has since removed any health threat and the pipes have been abandoned.

RC   RM -12
DUCK ISLAND: This is the name given the island by anglers and fishing guides. Waterfowl frequent this stretch of Glen Canyon especially during fall and spring migrations. Below Duck Island on river right is a gravel bar, commonly called Prop Bar, after the large number of outboard props damaged when river flows are low.

RR   RM -11.5
FERRY SWALE: Ferry Swale is described by some as an ancient meander of the Colorado River, perched above the canyon's floor. It is approximately five miles long and two miles wide. A swale is a low place which has moist, rank vegetation. A route leads down to the river from this hanging valley at River Mile -10. At the base of the cliff is the inscription "F.G. Faatz, Nov. 16, 1892." Faatz, who lived in Sanpete and Sevier counties in Utah, apparently traveled down the Colorado river for he also left his name, the name of his companion (known only by the initials W.H.E.), and the date August 27, 1892 in Cataract Canyon. It is not known at what point he and his companion, began or ended their journey. (18, 68)

RL   RM -6.5 to 61.5
NAVAJO INDIAN RESERVATION: The Navajo Nation follows the 1934 Treaty with the U.S. Government, in that their reservation extends to the center of the Colorado River. (128)

RL   RM -9.5
9 MILE DRAW: This draw, or small, natural drainage (usually at the upper part of a stream or valley) is nine miles above Lee's Ferry.

RL   RM -4
WATER HOLES CANYON: Water collects in pockets or holes in the canyon floor.

RL   RM -4
FINGER ARCH: This is a descriptive name for the thin, finger-like natural arch.

RC   RM -3.5
3 MILE BAR: This shallow, rocky bar is located about three miles above Lee's Ferry. It offers a challenge to navigation at low flows from the dam. At present, the deepest part of the channel follows a diagonal line through the stretch and not at the outside of the curve as the unwary boater would expect. Damaged motors and props are an expensive reminder.

RL   RM -3
CAVE CANYON: This is a descriptive name for the cave, or overhanging arch, located at the base of the cliffs. Under the recess on a rock, which has since fallen and is now upside down, is pecked the inscription "HISLOP 1889." John Hislop was a surveyor on both of the Stanton river-level railroad surveys in 1889-1890. River runners and historians, P.T. Reilly and Dock Marston call the cave, Hislop Cave. Traveling upstream in 1900, George W. James wrote, "To our right we saw the archway of an immense cave, -- a perfect Roman arch, covering a mouth of gigantic proportions. Some years ago a band of Navajos crossed into Utah, killed a Mr. Whitemore who owned a large band of sheep, and, it being winter and the river frozen over at Lee's Ferry, the Indians sprinkled sand upon the ice and drove the sheep into this cave for secure hiding. Since that time it has been the rendezvous of a noted band of horse thieves." (55, 94)

RL   RM -2.5

FALL CREEK: Origin unknown.

RL   AT RIM

ECHO PEAKS: From Lee's Ferry in 1871, Frederick Dellenbaugh climbed the summit of sandstone peaks where the wall of Glen Canyon breaks away to the southwest. He wrote, "I took it into my head to try to shoot from there into the water of Glen Canyon, beneath us, and borrowed Bishop's 44-calibre Remington revolver for the purpose. When I pulled the trigger I was positively startled by the violence of the report, a deafening shock like a thousand thunder-claps in one; then dead silence. Next, from far away there was a rattle as of musketry and peal after peal of the echoing shot came back to us. The interval of silence was timed on another trial and was found to be exactly twenty seconds. The result was always the same, and from this unusual echo we named the place Echo Peaks." The Southern Paiutes called the cliffs Skiwakavi. Early Mormon pioneers called it Hamblin Ridge. (32, 58)

RL   RM 0 to -3.5

STANTONS ROAD: The American Mining Law states that it is necessary to expend $100 annually on assessment work to keep a mining claim valid. In 1899, to protect his claims, Robert Brewster Stanton (1846-1922), an engineer by profession, built this dirt road. It is 10 ft wide and continues 1.5 miles above the ferry on river left. From 1897 to 1902, Stanton organized the largest mining venture to operate in Glen Canyon. He named the venture the Hoskaninni Mining Company after a Navajo chief who said that gold could be found along the Colorado River. The enterprise was a failure as the gold was too fine and passed through the dredges along with the sand and gravel. (29, 75, 87)

RL   RM -2

BUZZARDS HIGHLINE TRAIL: This faint trail descends the Echo Cliffs down the long, sandy slope to the river. Once an important Indian trail, one of Charles Spencer's men suggested the name after they were guided over the trail in May 1910 by a Navajo Indian. Perhaps they saw turkey vultures or felt that the waterless, steep trail provided easy pickings for the buzzards of the area. (87)

RL/RR   RM -1

UPPER FERRY SITE: This main ferry site operated from 1873 to 1928. In 1896, a track cable, attaching cables, and pulleys were

installed to aid the ferryboat across the current. Nearby are rock
foundations of cabins used by the ferrymen and travelers. (87)

RR   RM-0.5

THE CHARLES H. SPENCER: The steamboat *Charles H. Spencer*
was built by Charles Spencer in 1912 to carry coal from Warm Creek,
28 miles upstream, to Lee's Ferry. Spencer arrived at Lee's Ferry in
May 1910 to mine gold from the Chinle Shale cliffs behind Lee's Ferry
Fort. However, mercury in the amalgamator became clogged by an
unknown agent (later determined to be rhenium, a highly valuable super-
conductor for electricity) and gold could not be extracted. The steamboat was tied to the bank after only a few trips. The entire mining effort
failed and by 1913 everything and everybody associated with Spencer's
venture had gone. In 1915, high water lodged driftwood under the hull
causing it to list, the steamboat slid sideways into the river, and it sank
in a few feet of water. The broiler and main deck are still visible.
Spencer Canyon in lower Grand Canyon is named for another man by
the same name, who was a friend of the Hualapai Indians. (20, 87)

RR   RM 0

LEES FERRY FORT: John D. Lee had no connection with this
building. Jacob Hamblin ordered it built in June or July 1874 as a
means of keeping peace between the Navajo Indians of Arizona and the
Mormons of Utah. It was never attacked, but was used intermittently as
a residence, school, mess hall, and lastly as a trading post by Joseph L.
Foutz in the summer of 1877. "J. Hislop 1889" is inscribed near the
front doorway. Hislop was a civil engineer and surveyor with the
Stanton railroad survey. The Stanton crew had a Christmas dinner
beside the fort that same year. In 1910, Charles H. Spencer built an
addition onto the west end and converted the fort into a cook house for
his men. By 1913, the miners had departed and the addition was
partially torn down or collapsed. (87)

RR   RM 0

THE POST OFFICE: This small rock cabin located west of the fort
was used as a post office from 1879 to 1923. (87)

RR   RM 0

LEES FERRY: In 1858, Jacob Hamblin, with the help of Naraguts, a Paiute Indian, located the orginal site for Lee's Ferry[1]. The crossing was called Pahreah Crossing. In 1869, a group of Mormons built a stone building and a corral, calling it Fort Meeks, in honor of William Meeks, the elected leader of the camp. The fort was built to guard against marauding Navajos. (87)

The area was named after John Doyle Lee, Mormon pioneer and scapegoat. In 1858, Lee married Emma Batchelor (1836-1897), his 17th wife. Emma, an immigrant from England, had pulled a handcart from Iowa City to Salt Lake City the year before. The couple came to the area following orders from Brigham Young in December 1871. Emma called the area Lonely Dell. When the Lees served John Wesley Powell, Almon and Ellen Thompson, and Harvey De Motte watermelons after Powell's first expedition, Lee told Powell of Emma's name for the place and Powell adopted it and had it printed on the government maps. Today, the name refers to the ranch in the Paria River floodplain. Lee sometimes called the ferry, Saints Ferry (Saint is the name that Mormon Church members gave themselves), but it did not take. Lee and Emma farmed alfalfa, and supplemented their needs with apples, peaches, plums, and pears. (75, 87, 110)

Lee was called Yawgetts or cry-baby by the southern Paiute Indians, because he wept as he pled for the lives of the Fancher emigrants, then camped at Mormon Meadows in southwest Utah, while en route to California. Captain Charles Fancher and 11 families were massacred here in 1857. Indians killed women and older children and Mormons

---

[1]Over the years, the debate over the spelling of Lee's Ferry has raged. Should it be Lee's Ferry or Lees Ferry? And what about Lee Ferry? Many people feel that the latter two names are poor in grammar and history. The BGN has had a policy since the 1890s for omitting apostrophes before or after the possessive "s." The apostrophe is dropped as it could get "lost" in the map or be confused in charts with navigation symbols. Apparently, the apostrophe is not an element of grammar, but a symbol introduced during the 16th and 17th centuries to indicate the omission of one or more letters in a word. For example, "Lee, his ferry" was replaced in writing with an apostrophe "s" as Lee's Ferry. This, in turn, was shortened to Lees Ferry. The 1922 Coloraodo River Compact coined the word Lee Ferry (without the aposthrophe "s") to describe the political division between the Upper and Lower Basin States. (79, 87)

killed the men. Eighteen small children were not killed. The massacre grew out of the hysteria and war plans by the Mormons to keep out an invading United States army. In 1870, the Mormon Church officially excommunicated Lee when the Church was accused of harboring a fugitive and complicity in the crime. In 1877, twenty years after the crime, Lee was the only person tried and executed. However in 1961, Lee was reinstated with full membership and blessings in the Church of Jesus Christ of Latter-day Saints, the Mormon Church. (14)

Two years after Lee's execution, Emma sold her interests in the ferry to the Latter-day Saints Church. In 1879, she married Franklin H. French, a prospector. Franklin French was the miner who improved the Tanner Trail. Emma and Franklin eventually moved to Winslow where Emma was known as Dr. French for her nursing of expectant mothers. (15)

Since Lee spent much of his time as a fugitive from the authorities, the ferry was principally operated by Warren Marshall Johnson from 1875 to 1896, then by James S. Emett who sold it to the Grand Canyon Cattle Company in 1909. Coconino County operated the ferry from 1910 to 1928. The years 1876-1890 saw the most intensive use of the ferry, for it was the only river crossing for hundreds of Mormons heading into Arizona or young couples on their way to get married at the Mormon Temple in St. George via the "Honeymoon Trail." Outlaws, bank robbers, and bandits also crossed here. (87)

The 1923 Birdseye USGS Expedition established the custom of measuring river distances and naming features after mileages from Lee's Ferry. Colonel Claude Hale Birdseye, with a staff of ten engineers and boatmen, made an engineering survey from Lee's Ferry to Needles California using 18 ft wooden boats. (10, 11)

Lees Ferry is the official designation. On maps, the apostrophe is dropped, as this is the accepted convention in cartography. The ramp area at the Ferry is used for launching of commercial and private river trips downstream as well as up-river fishing and recreational boats.

A gaging station, operated by the USGS and built in 1921, is located in a narrow concrete stilling well on river left. Information on river stage and other physical parameters (temperature, pH, conductivity, dissolved oxygen) are transmitted to a satellite. Sediment collection and gage calibrations are made from the cableway with instruments dropped from a cable car. (12)

LEES LOOKOUT: This hill, atop the Shinarump conglomerate, is about 175 ft above and northwest of Lee's Ferry. An easy hike to the top yields a wonderful view of the Vermilion Cliffs, Paria River, and the Ferry area. Popular myth states that from this point, John D. Lee watched for Federal officers who he feared would arrest him. (87)

RL   RM 0

LEES BACKBONE: A road up this steeply inclined surface on the Shinarump conglomerate was used by Mormon emigrants continuously from 1873 to 1878, when a lower ferry site and dugway were constructed for use during low river flows. It could still be used during high flows, but was partially bypassed by a slightly better road over higher terrain in 1888. The road was abandoned in 1898 when the long dugway was opened. (87)

LONG DUGWAY: The long dugway, or road carved into the surrounding rock, was opened in 1898 and used until 1928. An 85,600 cfs flow on June 7, 1928, caused the ferry to capsize and snapped the track cable. Three men were killed: the trader Royce Dean, a Navajo passenger Lewis Nez, and the assistant ferryman Adolf Johnson, the young nephew of Warren Johnson who operated the ferry. (87)

RL/RR   RM 1.5

LOWER FERRY SITE: This site was used from 1878-1896 during low water stages of the Colorado River from August to May. The site was abandoned in 1896 when the upper ferry was anchored to a track cable. (87)

RR   RM 0.8

PARIA RIVER: Fray Francisco Atanasio Domingues, leading a ten man expedition to find a route from Santa Fe to Monterey, visited the area on October 26, 1776. Fray Silvestre Velez de Escalante, who wrote a journal account of the trip, named the Paria River the Rio Santa Teresa (Saint Teresa) and the vicinity thereabouts San Benito Salispuedes. San Benito either means Saint Bartholomew or was the name of a habit that convicts were forced to wear by the Spanish Inquisition. Salispuedes means get out if you can. Both epithets reflect their ordeal in trying to complete the journey. Escalante also wrote that the area "has an agreeably confused appearance." They were unable to cross the river at this point and continued upstream in Glen Canyon to a crossing they called La Purisima Concepcion de la Virgen Santisima, later called El Vade de los Padres or the Crossing of the Fathers. (31, 87)

The word Paria has many origins and meanings. Generally it is reported that it comes from the Paiute word paria-noquint meaning elk water. Pa means water or spring, while ria means water-deer or elk. However, a 1899 recommendation translates it as meaning water-muddy. It was sometimes spelled Pahreah or Pahrea, after the abandoned Mormon settlement in the upper drainage which was inhabited from the 1860s to 1915. The Paiute word pah'reah used in connection with the Virgin River, means water that tastes salty. Historian and river runner, P.T. Reilly recommended that it be spelled Pahreah, as many people mistakenly use the sound close to the English word pariah, meaning outcast. (45, 90, 110, 116, 127)

The Paria drainage is more a small creek than a river. It typically flows at 30 cfs. The maximum recorded discharge was 16,100 cfs in 1925 and the minimum was 1 cfs in most years prior to 1931. Powell called the fast water from Lee's Ferry through Paria Riffle a "long, rocky, mad rapid" as it was over a mile long. At low water, this stretch continues to keep a motor boatman's attention. (12, 83)

> **JOHNSON POINT**: This point of land on the right-hand abutment of Paria Canyon was named in 1965, by P.T. Reilly after Warren Marshall Johnson, who operated the ranch at Lonely Dell and the ferry crossing from 1876 to 1896. Johnson built a trail up to this point in the 1880s to utilize the grazing on the plateau. He died in 1902. (87, 115)

RL/RR   RM 1 to 276.5
GRAND CANYON NATIONAL PARK: The division line between Glen Canyon National Recreation Area and Grand Canyon National Park begins at the Paria Riffle, though some maps place it downriver 4.5 miles at Navajo Bridge. The river right boundary generally follows the rim, while the river left boundary at the rim along the Navajo Indian Reservation is termed an Indefinite Boundary. 1934 litigation of the Navajo boundary placed it at the east or south bank except where there were prior withdrawals; such as those made in 1910 and 1912 when the state of Arizona placed the boundary 1/4 mile back from the bank of the river. (128)

The general region we know as Grand Canyon National Park has had many changes of federal ownership. It was first proclaimed a forest reserve in 1893, a game reserve in 1906, a National Forest in 1907, and a National Monument in 1908. After Arizona became a state in 1912, Grand Canyon became the 16th National Park under the direction of the Secretary of the Interior and the NPS on February 26, 1919. The boundaries were enlarged in 1927, 1969, and 1975. (54)

RC   RM 1.8
LEE FERRY OR COMPACT POINT: In 1922, the states having an interest in the water of the Colorado met and hammered out the Colorado River Compact which apportioned percentages of the flow within a ten year period. This agreement located this spot, located one mile below the Paria River and called Lee Ferry, as the dividing point between the Upper Basin states (Wyoming, Utah, New Mexico, and Colorado) and the Lower Basin states (Arizona, California, and Nevada). (54)

RR   AT RIM
VERMILION CLIFFS: Powell named the Vermilion Cliffs. He wrote in his account of September 13, 1869, "Starting, we leave behind a long line of cliffs, many hundred feet high, composed of orange and vermilion sandstones. I have named them 'Vermilion Cliffs.' When we are out a few miles, I look back and see the morning sun shining in splendor on their painted faces; the salient angles are on fire, and the retreating angles are buried in shade, and I gaze upon them until my vision dreams and the cliffs appear a long bank of purple clouds piled from the horizon high into the heavens." (83)

RL   AT RIM
CHOCOLATE CLIFFS: Powell also named these cliffs. He wrote in his account of September 13, 1869, "At noon we pass along a ledge of chocolate cliffs, and taking out our sandwiches, we made a dinner as we ride along." (83)

RR   RM 3
CATHEDRAL WASH: This is named for the butte above called Cathedral Rock, which is 3760 ft high. Cathedral Rock has been called Sunset Rock and Five Mile Point as it is about five miles from the ferryman's ranch in the Paria River drainage. (115)

> **LOWREY SPRING:** This spring at the base of the Vermilion Cliffs is named after David Crockett "Buck" Lowrey, a home-

steader and Indian trader. In the 1920s, he developed the spring, and was given a patent for the land in 1933. Buck and his wife Florence ran a trading post, now known as Marble Canyon Lodge, on the west rim of the Marble Canyon gorge. Lorenzo Hubbell had loaned Buck the money to operate the lodge, but when Buck couldn't repay the money, Hubbell took over the operation. In 1949, Kyle Bales bought the lodge. His daughter, Jane Foster, inherited the lodge in 1959 and now operates it. (37, 115)

RL   RM 4.0

CCC TRAIL: The Civilian Conservation Corps built this route in the 1930s to enable the Navajos to bring their livestock to the river. Haldane "Buzz" Holmstrom (1909-1946) used this route in 1937 on his solo, first trip down the Colorado River. He bypassed Lee's Ferry, planning to use Navajo Bridge to reach Marble Canyon to pick up supplies. Imagine his shock when he found the bridge spanning the canyon's precipice above. Buzz is credited with being the first to run all the rapids in Grand Canyon on his second trip in 1938 while rowing his wooden boat *Julius F.*, named after his sponsor J.F. Stone. He was accompanied by Amos Burg who took movies of the trip and rowed the 80 pound *Charlie*, the first, inflatable rubber raft to make the journey. (63, 153)

RL/RR   RM 4.5

NAVAJO BRIDGE: This steel arch bridge was started June, 1927 and completed January, 1929 at a cost of $385,000. It is 834 ft long, the main arch is 616 ft long, and the 18 ft roadbed is 467 ft above the low water stage. It was also called the Lee's Ferry Bridge and the Marble Canyon Bridge. The Mormon president suggested it be called the Hamblin Bridge for Jacob Hamblin , or Hamblin-Hastele bridge for both Hamblin and the Navajo Chief Hastele. As a compromise, it was named Navajo Bridge. Arizona Department of Transportation will build a new bridge 330 ft downstream, styled after the original bridge, in the 1990s. Historic Navajo Bridge will remain as a foot bridge for visitors. (39, 75, 87)

RL/RR   RM 1 to 60

MARBLE CANYON: Powell wrote, "We have cut through the sandstones and limestones met in the upper part of the canyon, and through one great bed of marble a thousand feet in thickness. In this, great numbers of caves are hollowed out, and carvings are seen which suggest architectural form, though on a scale so grand that architectural terms belittle them. As this great bed forms a distinctive feature of the canyon, we call it Marble Canyon." The great bed of marble was the Redwall Limestone which when it is exposed at river level is polished by the Colorado River and resembles marble. The canyon was first called Marble Gorge and today is defined as the 60 mile section from the mouth of the Paria River to the mouth of the Little Colorado River. BGN 1925, 1960. (32, 83)

RR   RM 7.5
BADGER CREEK: Jacob Hamblin killed a badger in this drainage, then took it to the next creek downstream (Soap Creek) and put it in a pot over a fire to make stew. Next morning, he had a kettle of soap resulting from the alkalin water and the fat from the badger. The Southern Paiutes called this Tiraupankwicic or level ground-water running. It has also been called Clear and Spring Creek, though today it is generally dry. (45, 58, 110)

Jacob Hamblin, the "Leather-stocking Scout" or the "Buckskin Missionary", was sent by Brigham Young to explore the surrounding country in southern Utah and northern Arizona from the 1850s to 1870s. He lived near Mountain Meadows, Utah. He reported seeing the Ives Expedition in 1858. In 1862, President Brigham Young sent him to the Hopi villages to guide some of the Indians to a conference in Salt Lake City. He traveled south from Utah, crossed the Colorado River at the mouth of Grand Wash Cliffs, and then returned to Utah by way of the Crossing of the Fathers, thus making the first recorded round trip around the Grand Canyon. He is credited with locating the sites of Pearce and Lee's Ferry. Jacob Lake, Jacob Pools, Hamblin Ridge, and Hamblin Creek are named after him. (45, 54, 104)

RL   RM 7.5
JACKASS CREEK: Origin unknown. A jackass is a male donkey or burro. Burros were released in Grand Canyon by prospectors in the late 1800s to early 1900s. The animals were not native to the area and when their numbers increased, they competed with bighorn sheep and mule deer for food and water. Wild burros were removed by the NPS in the late 1970s. (54)

10 MILE ROCK: This piece of Toroweap Limestone in the channel marks this spot which is ten miles below Lee's Ferry. Les Jones' 1962 roll map labels this Slab Rock. (145, 152)

SOAP CREEK: This is the drainage where Jacob Hamblin made a kettle of soap by boiling a fat badger in alkaline water. The Southern Paiutes called this Sovinokwicic or cottonwood running. (45, 54, 58)

BROWN INSCRIPTION, BROWNS RIFFLE, AND BROWNS COVE: Frank Mason Brown was the president of the Denver, Colorado Canyon, and Pacific Railroad Company. In 1889, chief surveyor Robert Brewster Stanton, 14 men, and Brown embarked on a survey down the Colorado River from Green River, Utah. The purpose of the trip was to survey a river-level train route from western Colorado to the deserts below the Grand Canyon, from which coal could be transported to Los Angeles. Brown was drowned just below Salt Water Wash when the boat he was rowing and Harry McDonald was steering tipped over in a whirlpool. An inscription, etched by Peter Hansbrough on the left wall reads, "F.M. Brown, Pres. D, CC & PR was drowned July 10, 1889 opposite this point." P.T. Reilly, river runner and historian, suggested the names Brown's Riffle and Brown's Cove, in 1974. (94, 118)

SALT WATER WASH: This is a descriptive name for the salty or alkaline water to be found in the wash. Salts, such as calcium carbonate, sodium carbonate, and sodium sulfate, accumulate in desert soils and on rocky terraces.

> **SALT WEED BENCH:** This is named after the plant commonly called shad scale, a member of the Goose Foot Family, which grows on the dry mesas and slopes and can tolerate salty, alkaline soil.

SHEER WALL RAPIDS AND TANNER WASH: The 1923 USGS Expedition named this rapid. C.H. Birdseye, Chief of the Party, wrote that they could not climb around the rapid due to the sheer nature of the walls. The drainage is named after Seth B. Tanner, a Mormon pioneer who followed the upper part of the drainage along the Echo Cliffs from

Lee's Ferry to Tuba City and settled there. Tanner also prospected in eastern Grand Canyon. Early maps of the area call it Roundy Wash for Mormon Bishop Lorenzo W. Roundy, who drowned while attempting a crossing at Lee's Ferry in May, 1876. The other high placed Mormon officials, including Jacob Hamblin, made it to shore as did the ferryman Warren Johnson. (10, 87, 117)

On New Year's Day 1890, below Sheer Wall Rapid on Stanton's second trip, Franklin A. Nims, the expedition photographer, fell, broke his right leg, and was knocked unconscious. See Rider Canyon for the story of his evacuation. (94)

> **AH HOL SAH:** This is a Navajo word meaning hole, in reference to the sink or crater hole in the Kaibab Formation at the top of the drainage. (129)

RL   RM 16.5
HOT NA NA WASH: Hot Na Na is a Navajo phrase meaning to bubble over or something going over, as in a waterfall. Some topographic maps label this drainage as Hanaa Ninadzidzahi, a Navajo phrase which may mean coming over the hill again or once more. (129)

RM RR   RM 17
RIDER CANYON AND POINT AND HOUSE ROCK RAPIDS: This canyon is named for Rowland W. "Roy" Rider (1890-1984) by members of the 1909 Stone Expedition. Rider, a cowboy on the Kaibab Plateau, had many inventions to his credit (a rotary engine and a disposable hypodermic needle) and was a great story-teller. His tales as told to his granddaughter in *The Roll Away Saloon* are a treat and well worth reading. (85)

Eighteen year old Roy met Julius Stone's expedition when it passed Lee's Ferry on October 28, 1909. Stone had given money to James Emett, the Lee's Ferry ferryman, who was supposed to have bought food for Stone and his four men for ten days. Emett was gone and only three pounds of dried apples and half a pound of raisins could be found. Rider told Stone, "I believe the old cuss has kept the money and purposely forgot the supplies." Rider's account of the meeting varies a little. He said that Stone was ready to quit the expedition due to the dwindling food supplies, but that he urged them to continue as they could shoot bighorn sheep in the canyon below. Stone continued on and found instead, five domestic sheep near Soap Creek to add to his larder. (85, 98)

Earlier, there had been a range war between sheepman and cattlemen. The cattlemen cut dikes and two reservoirs so the sheep couldn't get any water. Ten thousand of the thirsty animals smelled water and plunged over the Marble Canyon precipice 740 ft to the river below. Their carcasses piled up and partially dammed the river. Emett's daughters rowed down and skinned the dead sheep for several days until the stench got to them, then rowed back to Lee's Ferry and sold the hides to the Navajos for jewelry and rugs. Apparently a few of the sheep survived to feed Stone's men. But, Emett was vindicated as an Indian came with supplies a few days after Stone left Lee's Ferry. (85)

Robert Stanton hiked out of Rider Canyon on his second trip in 1890 and walked 35 miles overland to Lee's Ferry to get help for Frederick Nims, the expedition photographer. The unconscious Nims, who was now off the payroll, was carried by stretcher out of the canyon and taken back to Lee's Ferry by wagon. Stanton assumed the photographic responsibilities for the rest of the trip and took over 1,600 pictures which, through rephotography, show both geologic and vegetational change over time. (94)

House Rock Rapids were named by C.H. Birdseye in 1923, who originally named the rapids "House Rock Canyon Rapids" for he thought it was the outlet of House Rock Wash. (10)

> **HOUSE ROCK VALLEY:** Frederick Dellenbaugh wrote in 1904, "A number of us were left for a while in camp in a valley lying between the Kaibab Plateau, then called Buckskin Mountain, and what is now called Paria Plateau, at a spring in a gulch of the Vermilion Cliffs. Two large rocks at this place had fallen together in such a way that one could crawl under for shelter. This was on the old trail leading from the Mormon settlements to the Moki country, travelled about once a year by Jacob Hamblin and a party on a trading expedition to the other side of the river. Somebody on one of these trips had taken refuge beneath this rock, and on departing had written, in a facetious mood, along the top with a piece of charcoal, Rock House Hotel... From this came House Rock Valley, and the name was soon a fixture, and went on our maps. And thus easily are names established in a new country." (32)

> **EMMETT WASH:** James Emett (spelled Emmett by the BGN) was a rancher and pioneer, who was given the assignment by the

Mormon Church to operate Lee's Ferry from 1896 to 1909. He kept his stock in House Rock Valley, had 18 children and two wives, and was the inspiration for Zane Grey's *Heritage of the Desert*. Grey described him as "well over six feet, and his leonine build, ponderous shoulders, and shaggy head and white beard gave an impression of tremendous virility and dignity." (87)

RC   RM 18.5
BOULDER NARROWS: This is named for the 30 ft diameter block of Toroweap Formation which has tumbled into the middle of the river. Driftwood from the last pre-dam high water in 1957 (estimated at over 125,000 cfs) is perched on top. (48, 82, 97, 145)

RR   RM 20.5
NORTH CANYON WASH: A descriptive name, as North Canyon flows almost parallel to South Canyon. The 1962 Jones roll map calls this 19 Mile Canyon (45, 152)

> **TATER CANYON:** In the late 1870s, members of the Mormon cooperative, the United Order or Orderville, tried to grow potatoes on the east side of the Kaibab Plateau. According to Warren Dart Judd, a 95 year old resident of Fredonia, the canyon got its name when a group of cowboys were frying potatoes in a skillet. They didn't watch them close enough and the spuds burned up. Thereafter, they called the canyon Tater Canyon.

> **BUFFALO RANCH:** A herd of about 90 buffalo, managed by Arizona Game and Fish Department, grazes the grassland in House Rock Valley. In 1906, "Buffalo" Jones, E.D. Woolley, and Uncle Jim Owens tried to breed a cross between buffalo and Galloway cattle, called a "cattalo", which they hoped would be more adapted to the western range and produce beef. The cross-breeding scheme failed. (54, 85)

                                                                          RM 20 to 30
ROARING TWENTIES: The rapids for the next 10 miles are spaced about one per mile and are collectively termed the Roaring Twenties, after the flapper era. C.H. Birdseye of the 1923 USGS Expedition gave many of the rapids in this section river mile designations for names.

INDIAN DICK RAPIDS: George C. "Black George" Simmons and Parkman "Parky" Brooks, two geologists and river guides, named this rapid after a July 1955 river trip with the Western Speleological Institute of Santa Barbara, California. Neither had navigated the canyon previously and they flipped in low water while floating ahead of the rest of the party. They swam to shore and righted their boat. After considering what had just happened to them and the pinnacle of Supai sandstone on the right side of the rapid, the term was minted. Simmons included the first formal publication of the name in the *River Runner's Guide to the Canyons of the Green and Colorado Rivers with Emphasis on Geologic Features: Marble Gorge and Grand Canyon.* Rumors that this stone tower is named after an Indian named Richard who kept lonely ladies company while their boyfriends and husbands were working on the river can now be dispelled. (135)

24.5 MILE RAPIDS: Albert "Bert" Loper, the Grand Old Man of the River, died here just short of his 80th birthday in 1949. His wooden boat was recovered and pulled upslope at Mile 41. His bones were discovered by a hiker in 1975 at Mile 70.5, near the mouth of Cardenas Creek. Loper was a boatman for a USGS survey on the San Juan River in 1921, the upper Green River in 1922, and Glen Canyon in 1939. The site was also erroneously called Tanner Rapids and Tanner Wash by the 1923 USGS Survey Expedition, who were not always able to correctly locate the mouths of tributary canyons. (3, 63, 92, 152)

25 MILE RAPIDS: Peter Hansbrough (boatman) and Henry Richards (cook's helper) of the Brown-Stanton expedition drowned here on July 16, 1889 after their boat collided with the overhanging cliff on the left side of the river. Neither were wearing life jackets as there were none on the trip. In 1974, P.T. Reilly suggested that the rapid be named Hansbrough-Richards Rapid, but the name has not been adopted. (94, 118)

CAVE SPRINGS RAPIDS: In 1923, C.H. Birdseye named the rapids Spring Cave Rapids for the springs and the cave. Here, in 1911, the Kolb Brothers found steel traps, old tools, and cooking utensils left by prospectors and trappers. Birdseye observed that the cave appeared to have been used since the Kolb trip. (10)

TIGER WASH: Origin unknown. This name may have been inspired by either the Redwall Limestone's light and dark bands of limestone and dolomite which alternate with chert, or the desert varnish at the mouth of the canyon. Both resemble tiger stripes. Desert varnish is a patina overlaying the rock which is built in successive layers like paint on a canvas and can take up to 10,000 years to develop. Water dripping over the rock evaporates and draws out manganese (birnessite) and iron oxide (hematite) from the rock. Rainshowers sweep atmospheric fallout, dust, or clay from the air which is cemented or "varnished" to the rock surface by the two minerals. The relative amounts of manganese and iron indicates the conditions under which the varnish was laid down. High manganese concentrations indicates a time of abundant moisture. Low manganese concentrations indicates dry conditions. The layers of desert varnish can be dated and give a record of climatic change in a desert environment. There is some evidence that bacteria fix these minerals and aid in the cementing of the varnish. Desert varnish can be made artificially by mixing manganese and iron oxide and is used to cover scars on petroglyph panels made by vandals. (8)

MNA RAPID: Museum of Northern Arizona scientists on an ecological survey were the first to observe the results of a rock fall which dropped rocks in the river while on a March 1974 river trip. They named the new rapid MNA after the museum in Flagstaff, Arizona.

SHINUMO WASH OR TWENTYNINE MILE CANYON: This wash is named for Shinumo Altar, a flat-topped mesa on the east side of the Marble Platform. Shinumo is a Paiute word meaning old people or cliff dwellers. Shinumo Creek is located at River Mile 108.5. (92)

> **SILVER GROTTO:** The 1968 National Geographic Society expedition named this grotto. (7)

> **SHINUMO ALTAR:** This feature was named by Frederick Dellenbaugh who sighted it from the Kaibab while triangulating in 1872. In describing it, he wrote, "It stood up so like a great altar, and, having in mind the house-building Amerinds who had formerly occupied the country, and whom the Pai Utes called Shinumo. I called it Shinumo Altar, the name it now bears. Probably there are people who wonder where the altar is from

which it was named. It was the appearance that suggested the title, not any archaeological find." Dr. Almon H. Thompson spelled the name Sheno-mo. Today it is pronounced as if spelled Shinamu. The Southern Paiutes called the mesa Tukwariri, or black hill. (32, 58)

SOUTH CANYON AND POINT: South Canyon is a descriptive term, named in conjunction with North Canyon. The two canyons run nearly parallel. After the deaths of Frank M. Brown, Peter Hansbrough, and Henry Richards, Stanton and his four men (John Hislop, George Gibson, Harry McDonald, and Frederick Nims) left the river by hiking out this canyon, calling the point on river left opposite the canyon, Point Retreat. The canyon is also known as Paradise Canyon, presumably after Vasey's Paradise below. In 1934, a skeleton was first reported by the Frazier-Hatch (The Dusty Dozen) river trip in 1934. The bones disappeared one by one and the skeleton no longer remains. (45, 63, 94, 152)

> **CLYDE EDDY CAVE:** This cave, located on river right, up-stream from the entrance to South Canyon was named for Clyde Eddy, organizer of a 1927 movie expedition. A plaque, placed in the cave by Fred C. Jayne, movie cameraman on a later expedition in 1934, has since been stolen by vandals. (92)

> **FENCE CANYON AND FAULT:** Fence Canyon is a descriptive name for an eight mile drift fence built north of it. The fence ran from the fault scarp (on the north side of House Rock Valley) to North Canyon. In 1908-1909 there was a range war between stockmen of the Kaibab Plateau and House Rock Valley. The Bar Z stock of 9,500 head, owned by B.F. Sanders of Salt Lake City were competing with the 6,000 head owned by smaller local ranchers. Two fences were built, one down the backbone of the Kaibab Plateau and another directly south from the Vermilion Cliffs to separate the pastures. Fence Fault crosses the Colorado River at Mile   (85)

> **WILDCAT CANYON:** Robert "Bob" Casbeer named this canyon when a mountain lion killed many sheep in a single night. (45)

STANTONS CAVE: This dry cave is named for Robert Brewster Stanton, whose 1889 expedition cached some of their gear in the cave before hiking out and returning to Lee's Ferry. In January 1890, he retrieved the following goods: flour, rice, sugar, coffee, sorghum, baking powder, photographic instruments, a revolver, and tobacco, and continued down the river. (84)

The cave is over 140 ft above the river and is about 140 ft deep. In 1934, Bus Hatch was the first to find split twig figurines. During excavation of the cave by Robert Euler in 1963, about 165 of these 4,000 year old willow hunting effigies were found. There was no evidence that the cave was lived in by pre-historic people. Buried in the cave's sediments were other prehistoric remains which pre-date the human users: a 15,000 year old teratorn, an extinct vulture larger than a condor; 20,000 year old extinct Harrington mountain goats; California condors, Humpback Chub fish, and horses. Driftwood which may have floated into the cave from a lake behind a rockfall dam downstream at Nankoweap Canyon was dated at about 43,000 years old. (40)

VASEYS PARADISE: Powell named this waterfall and associated greenery. In his account he wrote, "Riding down a short distance, a beautiful view is presented. The river turns sharply to the east and seems enclosed by a wall set with a million brilliant gems. What can it mean? Every eye is engaged, every one wonders. On coming nearer we find fountains bursting from the rock high overhead, and the spray in the sunshine forms the gems which bedeck the wall. The rocks below the fountain are covered with mosses and ferns and many beautiful flowering plants. We name it Vasey's Paradise, in honor of the botanist who traveled with us last year." George W. Vasey (1822-1893) accompanied Powell on his "Rocky Mountain Scientific Exploring Expedition" during the summer of 1868. He was a physician turned botanist who was an authority on grasses of the Southwest and Pacific slopes. Poison ivy abounds on the slopes, while above spelunkers have found over 2.5 miles of passageways in the Redwall Limestone solution caves. The flow of Vasey's Paradise Spring between 1923 and 1967 ranged from 0.1 to 10 cfs. The differences in flow is due to seasonal variations in the amounts of precipitation. (25, 83)

REDWALL CAVERN: Powell and his crew camped here on August 8, 1969. In his account, he wrote, "The water sweeps rapidly in this elbow of river, and has cut its way under the rock, excavating a vast half-circular chamber, which, if utilized for a theater, would give sitting to 50,000 people. Objection might be raised against it, however, for at high water the floor is covered with a raging flood." Powell exaggerated a little on the size, probably by a factor of ten. The NPS has placed this cavern in the Redwall Limestone off-limits to camping. (83)

NAUTILOID CREEK AND CANYON: In 1968, this name was suggested by geologist Troy Pewe for fossils of nautiloids (Rayonnoceras spp.), an extinct cephalopod related to present-day chambered nautilus, squid, and octopus. As the animal and shell grew, a small inner chamber was vacated. The void filled with air which enabled the organism to float. The fossils, first discovered and later described by geologist Bill Breed in 1967, can be seen in the floor of the slick rock grotto. The name was withdrawn for BGN approval in 1969 by Dr. Pewe as he thought it had been proposed earlier by geologists. The name sould be resubmitted for it is widely used by geologists and river runners. A variant spelling is Nautaloid. (7, 31, 48, 82, 127)

BRIDGE OF SIGHS: This natural bridge was named by the Kolb brothers for the bridge in Venice, Italy, through which prisoners were led for trial in the ducal palace. Ellsworth Kolb wrote, "Then came a gloomy, prison-like formation, with a 'Bridge of Sighs' two hundred feet above a gulch, connecting the dungeon to the perpendicular wall beyond; and with a hundred cave-like openings in its sheer sides like small windows, admitting a little daylight into its dark interior." (60)

TATAHATSO WASH: Tatahatso means big crevice in Navajo, tata means crevice. (129)

       LECHE-E WASH: This Navajo word means the color red. (129)

MARBLE CANYON DAM SITE: Between River Miles 32 and 40, the Bureau of Reclamation surveyed for a proposed Marble Canyon Dam

Site. Remnants of the survey work include drill sites to test the integrity of the rock, steel ladder supports, spoil (excavated rock), and bench marks and transect numbers painted on the walls. The proposed dams, including the Bridge Canyon Dam located below Diamond Creek, were intended to generate power which could be sold to pay for other water projects. If built, the Marble Canyon Dam would have backed up water to Lee's Ferry and the Bridge Canyon Dam reservoir would have reached Kanab Creek. A proposal by the City of Los Angeles called for a 42 mile tunnel under the Kaibab Plateau to divert water from Marble Canyon to Kanab Creek where hydroelectric power would be made as the waters rushed down into the Bridge Canyon reservoir. In 1966, David Brower, then Executive Director of the Sierra Club, mounted a campaign to stop the dam plans. In 1968, Congress heard the voices of the American people who wrote letters in unprecedented numbers to their representatives. Approval of the construction was denied and Congress placed a moratorium on the Federal Power Commission's right to sanction or study dams in the Grand Canyon. (54)

RR   RM 41
BUCK FARM: This canyon drains the eastern side of the Kaibab Plateau, also called the Buckskin Mountains. Buckskin is an anglicization of the Paiute word Bucksin, meaning mule deer. Indians and white settlers obtained large quantities of buckskin and today, mule deer are still to be found along the river. Buck Farm may refer to the abundance of deer in the area. The Jones roll map of 1962 calls this South Canyon. (45, 152)

RR   RM 41.5
BERTS CANYON: River runners call this unnamed canyon, Bert's Canyon, for Albert "Bert" Loper. Bert was just short of his 80th birthday on his second Grand Canyon trip (the first was in 1939). He died, perhaps of a heart attack, while rowing 24.5 Mile Rapid. His boat lodged on a rock bar on the upstream side of this canyon. His friends dragged it above the flood line and painted on the bow, "Bert Loper, Grand Old Man of the Colorado, Born: July 31, 1869. Died: July 8, 1949." (3)

RR   RM 41.5
ROYAL ARCHES: C.H. Birdseye, Chief of the USGS 1923 Expedition, wrote in his journal on August 9th, "Passed some beautiful arches in the right wall at mile 41.2. We named these the 'Royal Arches.'" (10)

ANASAZI FOOT BRIDGE: Gordon Denipah, a young Navajo damsite surveyor with the Bureau of Reclamation, first noticed this wooden platform during a helicopter ride in the 1960s. The bridge is under an overhang over 200 ft above the river at the base of the Redwall. Anasazi Indians built the bridge and used it as part of a cross-canyon trail connected with Eminence Fault downstream. (18)

PRESIDENT HARDING RAPIDS: This was named during the USGS Survey Expedition of 1923. C.H. Birdseye, Chief of the Party, wrote that they learned of President Warren Gamaliel Harding's death by radio at 8:15 Pacific Time (3/4 of an hour after it occurred) while at their camp at the head of Soap Creek Rapids on August 2, 1923. The broadcast said that August 10th was to be set aside as a Memorial Day, so the party decided to idle that day. Birdseye wrote in his journal on August 9th, "Camped on a sand bar on the left bank at the head of #19 Rapids which we named Boulder Rapids on account of a large boulder as big as a small house in the center of the channel. The entire force of the river seemed to drive towards this boulder and it looked bad." They lay idle on August 10th, out of respect to the memory of the 29th President of the United States. (10)

The rock in the middle of the rapid may have fallen about 1910. (152)

> **EMINENCE BREAK AND FAULT:** Origin unknown. Eminence is a word meaning a high place, hill, or elevation. The Eminence Break or Fault crosses the river here and an unmaintained trail follows the fault to the rim. (129)
>
> **TATAHOYSA WASH:** This is a Navajo word meaning hole in the crevice, tata means crevice. (129)
>
> **SMALL POINT:** This is probably a descriptive name for the point above. In the Navajo language, this would be called Dezhaa (point) Yazsh (small). (129)
>
> **SASE NASKET:** This is a Navajo word meaning either a sand dune or a stack of things. (129)

POINT HANSBROUGH: This point was named by Stanton for Peter Hansbrough who drowned in 25 Mile Rapid in 1889. Stanton wrote, "Ten miles below Point Retreat, as we went into camp one evening, we discover the body of Peter M. Hansbrough, one of the boatmen drowned on our trip last summer. His remains were easily recognized from the clothing that was still on them. The next morning we buried them under an overhanging cliff. The burial service was brief and simple. We stood around the grave while one short prayer was offered, and we left him with a shaft of pure marble for his headstone, seven hundred feet high, with his name cut upon the base; and in honor of this memory we named a magnificent point opposite -- Point Hansbrough." A second grave is also located opposite Point Hansbrough, that of David Quigley, a Boy Scout drowned in Glen Canyon about June 26, 1951. Don Harris, of the Harris-Brennon River Expeditions discovered the body on July 10 and dug a grave above the high water line. (55, 94, 128)

WILLIES CANYON: This unnamed canyon, located near River Mile 44.5, is sometimes called Willie's Canyon for Wilson Beigle "Willie" Taylor (see Willie's Necktie Rapid). In 1956, he accompanied Otis "Dock" Marston, Frank Masland, and Bill Beer with their three, aluminum, 30-hp boats. Willie died of a heart attack near President Harding Rapid and was buried here, high above the high water line. A memorial plaque on the Muav Limestone bench is his gravestone. Willie went on his first trip in 1949 and is credited with being the 100th person through the Grand Canyon after John Wesley Powell in 1869. (83, 133)

TRIPLE ALCOVES: C.H. Birdseye named these features in the Redwall Limestone. He writes in his journal of August 11, 1923, "Passed 3 large caves on the right bank at mile 46.5 which were beautifully arched and pillared. We called these caves 'Triple Alcoves.'" (10)

SADDLE CANYON AND MOUNTAIN: This drainage is located below Saddle Mountain at an altitude of 8,424 ft. The 1923 Birdseye USGS expedition called it Saddle Canyon. The name is also used on the 1926 Kaibab National Forest map. In the West, people call a pass between two peaks or hills a "saddle." The Saddle Mountain Burn of 1960 was the largest forest fire on the Kaibab Plateau. About 9,000 acres of timber were destroyed, of which 300 acres were within the Park boundary. BGN 1932. (10, 84)

COCKS COMBS: A series of sharp hills resembling a cockscomb, the fleshy, red part on the head of a rooster, give this area between North and South Canyon the name. BGN 1964. (45)

RR   RM 52
LITTLE NANKOWEAP CREEK AND CANYON: This smaller canyon is named after the larger Nankoweap Creek immediately downstream. BGN 1932. (45)

RR   RM 52.5
NANKOWEAP CANYON, CREEK, BUTTE, AND MESA: The Southern Paiutes called this Ninkuipi meaning Indians killed or people-killed, in memory of an incident in which Apache marauders who forded the Colorado River and came upon a Kaibab Camp at night. They hit each sleeping Indian on the head, killing all but one woman who escaped to Moccasin. This account agrees with information on file at the Grand Canyon, that an Indian, named Johnny, said that a fight between Indians took place at Big Saddle, near the head of Nankoweap. Other information states that Nankoweap is a Paiute word meaning singing or echo canyon. Dellenbaugh said Powell gave the creek this name on his second trip because of the deep echo heard in the canyon. Nankoweap Mesa was named by the NPS and Francois E. Matthes in 1927. BGN 1927, 1932. (33, 45, 58, 110)

Powell supervised the construction of the Nankoweap Trail so that Charles Doolittle Walcott's geologic expedition of 1882-83 could take horses and equipment into eastern Grand Canyon. Walcott studied the Grand Canyon Series of rock and later became Powell's successor as Director of the USGS. The trail followed an old Indian route. It was later used by prospectors, horse thieves, and Prohibition moonshiners. (54)

Deer on the South Rim used to be rare at the turn of the century. In 1924, the state of Arizona tried to organize a deer drive from the Kaibab Plateau, down the Nankoweap Trail, across the river, and along the Horsethief Trail to the South Rim. Hundreds of cowboys and Indians were hired to deliver 10,000 of the wild deer at one dollar per head. Needless to say, the effort was a grand failure. (54)

BOUNDARY RIDGE: This ridge is the boundary between Grand Canyon National Park (west of Marble Canyon) and Kaibab National Forest's North Kaibab Ranger District, thus the name. A variant name is Saddle Mountain. BGN 1927. (45)

BARBENCETA BUTTE: This butte, just above the mouth of Nankoweap Creek was named by Powell for Barbenceta, a friendly and principal chief of the Navajo Indians who made peace with Jacob Hamblin in 1870. He also aided the second Powell expedition in 1871. Varient spellings are Barbencita and Barbeneeta. BGN 1932. (45)

TILTED MESA: This descriptive name was given by Francois Matthes as it is a sloping tableland along the Kaibab Monocline. George Wharton James called it Tilts. BGN 1927. (45)

MARION POINT: Will C. Barnes, historian and place names researcher, named this point for John H. Marion (1835-1891) who published the Prescott *Arizona Miner*. BGN 1932. (45)

SEIBER POINT: This point was also named by Will C. Barnes for Al Sieber (1844-1907, spelled Seiber by the BGN). He was in charge of Apache scouts and led campaigns against almost every hostile tribe in the Arizona territory during the Indian wars from 1871-1886 for General Crook. Sieber was called Iron Man by the Apache. He was killed while overseeing construction of Theodore Roosevelt Dam when a boulder crushed him. BGN 1932. (45, 64)

WOOLSEY BUTTE: This point was named for King S. Woolsey (1832-1879), an Arizona pioneer, rancher, mule driver, and road builder who was active in territorial politics and had a reputation as an Indian fighter. He was a friend of Juan Chiavria, a friendly Maricopa Indian chief. BGN 1932. (45)

BOURKE POINT: Will C. Barnes also named this point for Lt. John G. Bourke, a writer, soldier, and historian, who came to Arizona in 1869. He was an aide to General George Crook in the 1870s and wrote several books about Arizona. BGN 1932. (45)

POINT IMPERIAL: This is the highest point overlooking the Grand Canyon (8803 ft), the fact which may have earned it the name. When Sharlot Hall visited it in 1911, it was called Skiddoo Point. Of the view to the east she wrote, "No words can tell how weird and unearthly it looks, much as the moon may be, for to the southern edge the round crater cone of Black Butte (now called Shadow Mountain) stands out against the brighter color so distinct that the purple mirage around it seems almost like volcanic smoke." Joseph Wood Krutch reported that a tree with the inscription "USGS Sept. 3, 1880" is at the point. BGN 1932. (45, 47, 61)

KOLB ARCH: This natural arch was first discovered in 1871 by Joe Hamblin, a horse packer for Powell. It was rediscovered in 1953 by Barry Goldwater, who then visited it by helicopter a year later. Goldwater nominated it to be named for Emery Clifford Kolb (1881-1976) in 1955. Emery and his brother Ellsworth made two trips through the Grand Canyon as well as hundreds of explorations. They are best known for the thousands of scenic pictures taken of the Grand Canyon and its visitors. A variant name is Kolb Bridge. Technically, an arch or window is an opening in a wall of rock along a joint, while a bridge is an opening created by water along a stream meander. Furthermore, a bridge usually spans a stream or dry wash. BGN 1977. (45)

MOUNT HAYDEN: Charles Trumbull Hayden (1825-1900) established a flour mill and operated a ferry across the Salt River, near Phoenix. The community which grew up around the mill was called Hayden's Ferry, but the name was changed to Tempe in 1879, a name proposed by B.P. Duppa. Hayden's son became Arizona's senior senator from 1912-1969. The peak located below Point Imperial was named by Frank Bond, who served as the Chairman of the BGN in 1932. BGN 1929. (45)

SULLIVAN PEAK: Will Barnes named this peak for Arizona pioneer Jerry W. Sullivan (b. 1844) who was a noted cattle rancher, Indian fighter, banker, and state legislator in Prescott. BGN 1932. (45)

HANCOCK BUTTE: This is named for Capt. William Augustus Hancock (1831-1902) who first came to Arizona in

1865. He surveyed the townsite of Phoenix, built its first house in 1870, and served as the first sheriff of Maricopa County. BGN 1932. (45)

KIBBEY BUTTE: Joseph Henry Kibbey (1853-1924) was a distinguished jurist and authority on Arizona water law. He was appointed to the Arizona Supreme Court but resigned to become the Territorial Governor from 1905-1909. Frank Bond suggested the name in 1929. BGN 1932. (45)

EHRENBERG POINT: This is named for Herman Christian Ehrenberg, a German mining engineer and surveyor who emigrated to Arizona. He founded a town in Yuma County and was killed in 1866 on the road to La Paz from San Bernadino, California. BGN 1932. (45)

SWILLING BUTTE: Jack (or John) W. Swilling (1831-1878) was a Texas Ranger and a member of the Second Walker Expedition. He built the Tempe Canal in 1871, the first irrigation canal utilizing the waters of the Salt River. Unfortunately, Swilling had the habit of confessing to crimes he didn't commit when he was inebriated. Because he claimed to have robbed a stage and committed murder, he was sentenced to the Yuma Penitentiary where he died. He was later found innocent. BGN 1932. (45)

DUPPA BUTTE: Bryan Philip Darell Duppa (1832-1892), a well educated and adventuresome Englishman, killed a fellow officer in a duel. He emigrated to Arizona and became a pioneer in the Salt River Valley in 1863, where he was sometimes referred to as Lord Duppa. He was a partner with Jack Swilling in the irrigation canal business. He proposed the names for Phoenix (based upon classical mythology) and Tempe (for its similarity to the countryside by the Vale of Tempe in Greece). BGN 1932. (45)

NOVINGER BUTTE: Pioneer Simon Novinger (1832-1904) lived in the Salt River Valley in the early 1870s. BGN 1932. (45)

ALSAP BUTTE: John T. Alsap (1832-1886), "The Father of Maricopa County," was a county and district attorney and a probate judge. BGN 1932. (45)

FARVIEW: From this point a broad view of the Painted Desert can be seen. (45)

RR   RM 53

ANASAZI GRANARIES: The Pueblo Anasazi Indians planted corn, beans, and squash on the riverine terraces and stored the seed crop in the storeroom granaries located in the cliffs about 600 ft above the river. One of the doorways was damaged by a visitor in 1980 who must have steadied himself by placing hands on both sides and peering into the opening. The door was restored, but please look carefully. (11)

RL   RM54.5

GRAY CASTLE: Origin unknown.

RR   RM 56

KWAGUNT CREEK, CANYON, VALLEY, AND BUTTE: Powell named this place for a Paiute Indian named Kwagunt (Quawgunt or Kwaganti, a Southern Paiute name meaning quiet or quiet man), but he was also known as Indian Ben. He told Powell that he owned the valley, for his father had given it to him. He discouraged visitors, as he wanted to keep the sage seeds which were available there for himself. One story reports that he escaped to the valley when trying to hide from Apache raiders, while another states that as a child, he and his sister where the only survivors of an attack by Yavapai Indians on his family's band camped on the Kaibab Plateau. The children made their way to another band camped by Kanab Creek. Later, this tributary to Kanab Creek, was named Kwagunt Hollow for him. BGN 1906, 1927. (42, 43, 45, 58)

ATOKO POINT: Origin of meaning and naming unknown. A different spelling, Atoka, is the name of a county and county seat in Oklahoma named for a Choctaw sub-Chief Atoka and Captain Atoka a famous Choctaw ball player. The word is from the Choctaw word hitoka or hetoka, meaning ball ground. BGN 1906.

GUNTHER CASTLE: Gunther, the King of Burgundy, in the great German Nibelungen epic, was the brother of the beautiful princess Kriemhild and husband of Brunhild, the princess of Issland.

GALEROS BUTTE: Juan Galeros was one of three men from the Cardenas Expedition in 1540, who tried to the reach the Colorado River from the South Rim. The men returned due to lack of water after penetrating the canyon only a third of the way. BGN 1932. (54)

SIEGFRIED PYRE: Siegfried was a prince of the lower Rhine who captured the treasure of the Nibelungs (the hoard had the property that no matter how much was taken from it, the quantity was never less), slayed the Dragon of the Lindentree, and won Brunhild for King Gunther. Using his magic cloud cloak which made him invisible, he tricked Brunhild, who vowed only to marry the man who could surpass her in jumping, throwing a stone, and casting a spear. Siegfried was killed by Hagen, who discovered that the only spot where he could be injured was between the shoulder blades. The burning of Siegfried's funeral pyre forms the spectacular climax to the opera, *Der Gotterdammerung*. BGN 1906.

HARTMAN BRIDGE: The second largest natural bridge in Grand Canyon (after Alamo Arch at Fern Glen) is named for James Hartman, a charter pilot who first saw it from the air. (131)

HUTTON BUTTE: Oscar Hutton (1830-1873) was a military man (Company F, Arizona Volunteers 1865-66), Indian fighter, interpreter, guide, and packer. He was reputed to have killed more Indians than any other man in Arizona. Oscar had six toes on each foot and was killed when a mule kicked him in the face. BGN 1932. (45)

TRITLE PEAK: Frederick A. Tritle was Arizona's territorial governor during the 12th Legislature in 1883. He was a mining expert and developed the Jerome Copper Mine. The peak was named by Will C. Barnes. BGN 1932. (45)

COLTER BUTTE: James G.H. Colter (b. 1844 in Nova Scotia) settled along the Little Colorado River near Springerville in 1872. He was a freighter and an Indian fighter of Apache Indians and outlaws. BGN 1932. (45)

JEFFORDS POINT: Thomas Jeffords (1832-1914) was a red headed pioneer, Indian trader, ex-soldier, stage driver, and government scout. He was a personal friend of Cochise, the Chiricahua chief, who called him Chickasaw (Brother) or Toglito (Blood Brother). Jeffords arranged a peace with Cochise in 1870, thus preventing a battle. He served as the first Indian Agent to the Chiricahua Indian Reservation. BGN 1932. (45)

BANTA POINT: Albert Franklin Banta (1846-1924) was a scout for General George Crook (1865-1871) and for the Wheeler Expedition from 1871-1873. He was adopted by the Zuni Indian tribe in 1866. He later served as an attorney, judge, and legislator and is called the Father of Apache County. He told tall tales and claimed to have been everywhere in Arizona. BGN 1932. (45)

COCHISE BUTTE: Cochise (d. 1874) was the chief of the Chiricahua Apaches. He led the resistance to the white settler's incursions into their lands in the 1860s. BGN 1932. (45)

BRADY PEAK: Peter R. Brady was a Texas Ranger, Arizona pioneer, miner, and territorial senator. BGN 1932. (45)

VISTA ENCANTADA: Vista Encantada is Spanish for enchanting view. It is the name found on most topographic maps. However, Vista Encantadora is sometimes used. In 1941, then Park Superintendent Bryant suggested it be changed to Encatadora because encantada is not grammatically correct. BGN 1924. (45)

RR   RM 57.5

MALGOSA CANYON, CREEK, AND CREST: These features are named for Pablo de Melgosa (spelled Malgosa by BGN), one of Cardenas' "lightest and most agile men." Melgosa, Juan Galeros, and another companion attempted to climb down to the Colorado River from the South Rim in 1540. The explorers only got about a third of the way down along a ridge in a day before they turned back. BGN 1906, 1927. (54)

AWATUBI CREEK, CANYON, CREST: Francois E. Matthes proposed this name. Awatubi (Awatobi or Awatovi) is a Hopi word meaning high place of the bow people. Awatubi was an ancient Hopi pueblo village, located in the Painted Desert six miles west of Jeddito and 75 miles north of Holbrook. It is one of the original villages of the Tusayan visited by Tovar and Cardenas in 1540. The San Bernadius Mission, built there in 1629, is credited with being the first building erected by Europeans in Arizona. The town and the mission were destroyed in 1700 by neighboring pueblos who disliked the inhabitants for their friendly feeling for the Spanish. BGN 1906, 1927. (39, 45)

BLUE MOON BENCH: This broad expanse north of the Little Colorado River on the Navajo Indian Reservation may be named after Blue Canyon (also known as Moenkopi Wash) which drains Black Mesa and enters the Little Colorado River. Blue Canyon is named after the hazy blue color of the canyon walls. A blue moon is defined as the second full moon in a month. On an average, this happens every 2.7 years. A 1900 map calls this bench the Carson Plains, presumably after Kit Carson (1809-1868), a frontiersman and scout. Other maps label it as Tusayan National Forest (39, 45, 152)

DESERT FACADE: A descriptive name, a facade is the principal front of a building or any other face of a building which has been given special architectural treatment. BGN 1906.

CHUAR BUTTE: Chuar is a shortened form of Chuarrumpeak, a young, Kaibab Paiute chief. Jacob Hamblin introduced Chuar to John Wesley Powell to discuss the death of Powell's men killed on the Shivwits Plateau in 1869. He was called Frank by the early settlers and Chuar by his own people. The butte was formerly called Hercules Hill. BGN 1906. (45)

A Trans-World Airlines Constellation and a United Airlines DC-7 collided at 21,000 feet over Chuar Butte on a reasonably clear day about noon on June 30, 1956 while on eastward flights from Los Angeles. All 128 persons aboard were killed and the debris fell over Temple and Chuar Buttes. Many of the victims were buried in the Grand Canyon and Flagstaff cemeteries. The last remains of victims and debris were removed in the late 1970s. The crash resulted in an act which established the Federal Aviation Administration in 1958. A small canyon downstream two miles, between Chuar and Temple Buttes, is sometimes called Crash Canyon by river guides. (54)

RL   RM 61.5

LITTLE COLORADO RIVER: At one time the Little Colorado River was called Tol Chaco by the Navajos, meaning Red Stream or Red Water. The Havasupais call it Ahaka-thiela meaning Salty River. Cardenas called it the Rio del Lino, or Flax River, because of the wild flax growing on its banks. In 1604, Juan Mateo de Onate, New Mexico's first governor, used the word colorado (or red) for the Little Colorado River. Fray Francisco Garces saw it on June 28, 1776, calling it both the Rio Jaquesila (Unruly River) de San Pedro and the Rio San Pedro (River of Saint Peter). In 1854, Lt. Amiel W. Whipple saw it and reported that it was called the Flax River and Colorado Chiquito. Ives also used that name in 1861. (4, 45, 65)

Powell called it the Rio Colorado Chiquito or Little Red River. John Colton Sumner, who navigated Powell's head boat, referred to it as the Rio del Lino, or Flax River, a name rarely used. Powell wrote in his journal of August 10, 1869, "At two o'clock we reach the mouth of the Colorado Chiquito. This stream enters through a canyon on a scale quite as grand as that of the Colorado itself. It is a very small river and exceedingly muddy and saline." Other variant names include Colorado Chiquita. BGN 1891. (24, 83)

The gorge of the Little Colorado River is very steep-walled. Because of the dramatic chasm, cowboys in the area used to call it Poison Canyon, since one drop would kill you. Today, river runners sometimes call it by its initials, the LCR. The gorge begins about nine miles below Cameron, 41 miles above the confluence. (100, 130)

The 107 mile long Little Colorado River has its headwaters in the White Mountains of Arizona. At Cameron, the flow ranges from no flow to an average of 240 cfs. Maximum discharge can reach about 25,000 cfs, though a discharge of 120,000 cfs occurred during September 1923. Much of the water is diverted for irrigation above Cameron. Springs located about 10-13 miles above the confluence, the largest called Blue Spring, are perennial and the combined flow ranges about 220 cfs. However, smaller springs keep some water in the bed from 21 miles upstream to the confluence with the Colorado River. About 75% of the flow comes from the San Francisco Peaks volcanic field, while the remainder, estimated to be at least 20,000 years old, comes from Black Mesa basin aquifer on the Hopi and Navajo Reservations. (12, 25)

The endangered Humpback Chub (Gila cypha) is commonly found in the Little Colorado River, along with other native fish such as Bluehead Sucker, Flannelmouth Sucker, Razorback Sucker, and Speckled Dace. Exotic fish, such as Channel Catfish, various species of trout (Rainbow, Brook, and Brown), Carp, Fathead Minnow, and Rio Grande Killifish also prey on the native fishes or compete for resources. A new, voracious predator, the Striped Bass, has also been found at the confluence, at Lee's Ferry, and in the lower canyon from Deer Creek down to Lake Mead. (97)

The color of the turquoise waters, when not muddied by runoff, is due to the dissolved calcium carbonate in the water. Chloride is the dominant chemical found in the water, along with bicarbonate. Crystals of travertine are deposited when the dissolved carbon dioxide bubbles out of the water. The white, friable material which coats the bottom of the stream is called tufa. Tufa (not to be confused with tuff, vocanic ash or dust) is a thin, soft, spongy porous sedimentary rock of calcium carbonate. It may also be precipitated by algae or bacteria. The hardened terraces are travertine, which cements boulders and rocks and creates small falls and terraces along the Little Colorado River. A large fall, sometimes called Atomizer Falls for the water which is changed into a fine spray, is located upstream of Salt Trail Canyon. (25)

> **CAPE SOLITUDE:** This descriptive name has been used since the early 1900s to describe the solitary point which juts over 3,400 feet above the confluence with the Little Colorado River. The elevation at the rim is 6,146 ft. A 1900 map calls it Navajo Point and the unnamed point opposite was called Point Cardenas. Cape Solitude was called Cape Desolation by the Kolb brothers. BGN 1906. (45, 60)

> **BEAMERS CABIN:** Ben Beamer converted an abandoned Anasazi dwelling (noted by Powell in 1869) into his own one-room cabin when he came here in the winter of 1890 or 1891. He tried to support himself by farming and prospecting. (54, 83)

WALTER POWELL ROUTE: River runners have named this short, yet steep route, about two miles upstream from the confluence, for Captain Walter Henry "Old Shady" Powell (1842-unknown), Powell's younger brother. Walter got his nickname from a song he used to sing. He should not to be confused with Walter Clement Powell, Powell's orphaned cousin, who accompanied the second expedition. Captain Powell had spent ten months in a Confederate prisoner of war camp and his brother hoped that the rigors of the expedition's outdoor life would restore his psyche. Walter spent a day during the 1869 expedition hiking to the top and back with a barometer to ascertain the height of the canyon walls. (19, 83)

SIPAPU: Sipapu, or Sipapuni, is a Hopi word meaning Place of Emergence. It is the entrance to the underworld or World Below through which the Hopi people entered this (the fourth) world from the third world. A pregnant woman became stuck in the opening and that is why the Hopi Tribe is so small. Sprits return through this opeing after death. In a kiva, a symbolic sipapu is represented by a ceremonial small hole in the floor. The Sipapu, a travertine dome and spring, is located 4.5 miles upstream from the confluence. It is sacred to the Hopi Indians, who along with the NPS, have asked that it not be visited or observed. (106)

SALT TRAIL CANYON: Also called Owngtupka (Salt Canyon) by the Hopis and Bekihatso Wash (or Big Foot Wash) by the Navajo, Salt Trail Canyon was the trail used by the Hopi Indian clans from Third Mesa on the pilgrimage to the Hopi Salt Mines and other shrines. (38, 91, 99, 129)

BLUE SPRING: In the 1890s, this descriptive name for the color of the water issuing from the spring caused Dan Hogan, an early prospector and miner, to guide a party on horseback to the spring. He thought that the name might indicate an oil seep. (100)

PAINTED DESERT: The Painted Desert is the name given by Dr. Newberry, geologist on the Ives Expedition. He probably anglicized the Spanish name El Desierto Pintado, which was applied in 1540 for the vast treeless area of brilliantly colored sandstone. The Navajos call the Painted Desert Halchiitah,

meaning amidst the colors. There are no well-defined boundaries to the Painted Desert and most people consider Petrified
Forest National Monument to be the center. (33, 45)

RM 0 (or 62) to 277
GRAND CANYON: The Havasupai Indians called the Grand Canyon
Wikatata or Rough Rim.   They also referred to it as Chicamimi
Hackataia.   Chicamimi means large canyon, while Hakatai means any
large, roaring sound caused by a fierce wind or dashing water.   The
Hopi Indians call it Suukotupqa or Sakwatupqa meaning Big Canyon.
The Navajo Indians call the Grand Canyon, Bidahaztii. (55, 91, 129)

In 1540, Don Pedro de Tobar, Coronado's chief standard bearer, or
ensign, was perhaps the first foreigner to hear about the Grand Canyon.
He investigated the Hopi villages of Tusayan, to which the Zuni Indians
had directed the Spaniards on their quest for the fabled Seven Cities of
Cibola. Tobar was told of a great river not far to the west and of a land
inhabited by people with very large bodies, a reference perhaps to the
Havasupai who are generally larger than the Hopi. Whether he saw the
canyon is unknown. In August of that year, Garcia Lopez de Cardenas
was taken to the rim of the Canyon by the Hopis. (45, 54)

Fray Francisco Tomas Garces, a missionary and Spanish explorer,
visited the Hualapai, Havasupai, and Hopi Indians in 1776. He called
the Grand Canyon "Puerto de Bucareli" or Bucarel Pass after Antionio
Maria Bucareli y Ursua, then the viceroy of New Spain. He described
the canyon as a "calaboose of cliffs and canyons." Calaboose is from the
Spanish word calabozo, meaning prison or dungeon. (54)

In 1857, Lt. Joseph Ives called the canyon, Big Canyon. The name
Grand Canyon first appeared on an 1868 railroad survey map prepared
by General Wm. J. Palmer. The first mention in print of Grand Canyon
of the Colorado is attributed to Samuel Bowles, when he wrote of his
travels in the West in 1869. However, Powell is credited with the first
consistent and authoritative use of the name. After his first expedition
in 1869, he officially named Grand Canyon, defining it as the stretch of
the Colorado River from its confluence with the Little Colorado River.
Sumner, Powell's chief boatman and guide on his first trip, states that he
wanted to call it Coronado Canyon, but that, "Major Powell told me it
should bear my name if he got through and ever had the opportunity to
place it on the Government map. Well, he got through all right, but he
forgot his vows and named it the Grand Canyon." (24, 54,)

Today, Grand Canyon is defined as extending from the mouth of the Paria River and Lee's Ferry to the mouth of Grapevine Wash, near Pearce Ferry. Some people consider that it starts at the mouth of the Little Colorado River, where Marble Canyon is considered to end. But physiographically, Marble Canyon is part of Grand Canyon.

RR   RM 63
TEMPLE BUTTE: This descriptive name was submitted by the NPS. BGN 1932.

RL   RM 63.5
HOPI SALT MINES: These mines at river level are sacred to the Hopi Indians and the NPS have placed them off limits to visitation. The white stalactites and sheets of salt can be seen from the river. In 1912, Don Talayesva of Oraibi made a pilgrimage to the mines and an account of the trip is told in *Sun Chief, The Autobiography of a Hopi Indian* (edited by Leo Simmons). In 1956, Harvey Butchart rediscovered the route to the Hopi Salt Mines and Salt Trail Canyon. Following Butchart's directions, Fred Eiseman and three companions located the mines in 1958. The Hopis suspended trips to the salt mines by their people after theft of ritual masks in 1980. An analysis of the salt crystals, which form in long straw-like tubes, show them to be nearly pure sodium chloride. The white material on the cliffs leached of salt is almost pure calcite and gypsum. (16, 38, 99, 128, 131)

RR   RM 64.5
CARBON CREEK, CANYON, AND BUTTE: Carbon Butte was named by Charles E. Walcott due to its position between Carbon Creek and the Colorado River. The 1923 USGS Birdseye expedition named Carbon Canyon, probably for the carbon-colored exposures of the Cardenas Basalts. BGN 1906, 1927, 1932. (10, 45)

> **BUTTE FAULT:** This fault trends next to several buttes, thus the name.

RL   AT RIM, RM 64.5
PESHLAKAI POINT: This 6,302 ft point was named for Peshlakai Atsidi (1850-1939), a Navajo Indian, who was noted for his "clear analytical thinking; for a profound understanding of his fellow tribesmen and their problems; and for a truly statesman-like perspective on matters affecting their welfare." He was a highly respected leader of the Navajo

who lived at Black Point on the Little Colorado River. BGN 1977. (57, 127)

Pish-La-Ki was also the name for a lost silver mine near Navajo Mountain on the Utah/Arizona border. Legend had it that the Spanish enslaved Navajos to work the mine and the placer bars along the river. After the Spanish left, the mine was said to have supplied the Navajos with the silver they used for making jewelry. Pish is a corruption of the Spanish word peso meaning money or silver. Cass Hite, a prospector, was made a blood brother by the Navajo Chief Hoskanini, who called him called Hosteen Pishlaki, also meaning Mr. Silver or White Silver Hunter, in 1882-83. Hoskanini told Hite that gold could be found in White Canyon. Hite did find gold and first called the ford across the river, Dandy Crossing, poking fun at the other crossings used by Mormons such as Hole-in-the-Rock and Hall's Crossing. Hite settled downstream at Ticaboo Creek in Glen Canyon, but the community that grew up opposite the mouth of White Canyon on Trachyte Canyon, came to be called Hite. Hite was flooded by Lake Powell in 1964 and a marina, called Hite Marina, was created upstream opposite the Dirty Devil River, renamed the Fremont River. (3, 37)

RL   RM 65.5
PALISADES CREEK AND PALISADES OF THE DESERT:
Palisade is from the French word palissade which is derived from the Latin word palus meaning stake or wooden post used in sword practice. Palisades were a fence of stakes, pointed at the top and set close with others, and used to enclose or defend a fort or town. Later, the term was extended to describe this line of high, steep cliffs on the eastern rim of the canyon. This name was used by the USGS as early as 1886, probably following Major Dutton's description of the area. It was then submitted by Francois E. Matthes in 1902, who wrote that the cliffs rise, "in rhythmically spaced recesses and alternating humps and hollows which...produce a striking resemblance to a palisade." BGN 1906, 1932. (127)

> **McCORMICK OR TANNER MINE:** This copper and silver mine was discovered by Seth Tanner in 1890. George McCormick took over the mine in May 1903, naming it the Copper Blossom Mine. The McCormicks renewed mining activity during World War I. It is now known as the Tanner Mine. (130)

LAVA CANYON, CREEK, AND BUTTE: The creek, arising near Atoko Point, was named by the members of the USGS due to the presence of basalt in the area (technically lava is molton rock). In the 1930s it was known locally as Silver Creek. BGN 1906, 1930. (4)

> **CHUAR LAVA HILL:** A descriptive name for the basalt rock upstream of Lava Canyon.

> **CHUAR CREEK:** Chuar is a shortened form of Chuarrumpeak, chief of Kaibab Paiutes. Chuar was introduced to Powell by Hamblin in 1869. See Chuar Butte. BGN 1906, 1930. (45)

> **COPPER GRANT MINE:** The opening to this mine is visible from the river. (130, 132)

> **MORNINGSTAR MINE:** This mine is located up Lava Canyon about one mile and was discovered by Harry McDonald in 1890, who was on the Stanton-Brown railroad survey trip. A morning star is a bright planet, usually Venus, seen in the east before sunrise. (130)

> **NATCHI CANYON:** This canyon is named after Natchi, the son of Cochise, the great Chiracahua Apache chief, who succeeded his father in 1876. Natchi surrendered along with Geronimo, the Apache shaman and war leader, to General Miles in 1886. He was exiled to Florida with other Chiracahua Apache Indians. His name is also spelled Naji, Naiche, and Natchez. Nachi is also a Hopi word for the standard planted on a kiva during a ceremony. See Uncle Jim Point. BGN 1906. (45, 106)

> **NAJI POINT:** This is another spelling for Natchi. BGN 1906.

> **HUBBELL BUTTE:** This butte was named by Will C. Barnes for Juan Lorenzo Hubbell (1853-1930), prominent Indian trader, who established Hubbell Trading Post, now a National Monument on the Navajo Indian Reservation. He also served as Coconino County sheriff and as a member of the 17th Territorial Government and State Senate. BGN 1932. (45)

POSTON BUTTE: Charles DeBrille Poston (1825-1902) was a pioneer, lawyer, superintendent of Indian Affairs (1863), First Territorial Delegate to Congress from Arizona (1864), and Register, U.S. General Land Office. He is called the "Father of Arizona," for encouraging members of Congress to pass a bill, later signed by President Abraham Lincoln, that created the Territory of Arizona. BGN 1932. (45)

CHIAVRIA POINT: Juan Chiavria, a Maricopa chief, was at the battle of Bloody Tanks. Chiavria's and King S. Woolsey's men massacred a group of visiting Apaches whom they had invited into their camp and whom they thought were hostile. (45)

RL   RM 67
ESPEJO CREEK AND BUTTE: The creek and butte are named by Frank Bond for Antonio Espejo, Spanish explorer, who visited northern Arizona in 1582-83 with Father Bernardino Beltran. They crossed the Colorado River about 55 miles northeast of Grand Canyon as the Crossing of the Fathers (El Vado de los Padres). Espejo in Spanish means mirror or windowpane. Espejo called the region of the Hopi villages, Mohoce and mentioned five pueblos. Mohoce was rendered by the Spanish into Moki and Moqui. The Hopi word Moki means means variously green, blue, or blue-green; desirous of or in need of; a sack full; or deer. Mokee means dead. (45, 91)

RL   RM 67.5
COMANCHE CREEK AND POINT: The Comanche are a tribe of Plains Indians feared by the Pueblo Indians. The point had earlier been called Bissel Point for an early official of the Atchison-Topeka and the Santa Fe Rail Road. BGN 1906, 1932. (44, 45, 55)

RL   AT RIM
DESERT VIEW: In 1906, this viewpoint was called Navajo Point. It was renamed in 1932 for the view of the desert below. (70)

THE WATCHTOWER: This structure was built at the end of the East Rim Drive in 1932. Designed by architect Mary Jane Colter, it was built using native stone around a steel framework. The logs in the Kiva Room were salvaged by Colter from the two story, log cabin Grandview Hotel built by Pete Berry in 1897. It is decorated inside by Hopi Indian artists with replicas of ancient petroglyphs and kiva paintings. The Navajo refer to the watchtower as Yahehahi or standing tower. Colter also designed Bright Angel Lodge, Lookout Studio, Hermits Rest, and Phantom Ranch. (54)

CEDAR MOUNTAIN: This is a descriptive name for the "cedar" trees, actually a species of Juniper, which grow on the slopes. BGN 1906. (45)

RL/RR   RM 68 to 72

FURNACE FLATS: Furnace Flats is the name given by river runners, hikers, and locals to this open, passive solar collecting, Dox Sandstone stretch from Tanner to Unkar Rapids. Furnace-like temperatures nearing 140 degrees F at the surface can be measured on summer days. The sun rises early and sets late.

RL   RM 68.5

TANNER CANYON, TRAIL, AND RAPIDS: Seth B. Tanner, a Mormon settler at Moenkopi, Arizona in 1875, was a trader and mining pioneer. He was Chairman for the Little Colorado Mining District in 1880, which covered a large area south and east of Grand Canyon and found minor copper mines near the river. To reach his mines, he reconstructed an old Indian trail from the South Rim to the Colorado River in 1884 or 1885. (54, 130)

The Tanner Trail crossed the Colorado River above the Little Colorado River and went out the north side near Saddle Mountain. The trail was also called the Horsethief Trail, as it was said to be used by a gang who stole horses in Utah and Arizona. It was also used as an outlet for illegal booze during Prohibition. Robert Stanton reported that he met a Flagstaff prospector, Felix Lantier, at the base of the Tanner Trail in February 1890. (54, 94)

The Tanner Trail has also been called the Tanner-French Trail. Franklin French, desiring to do some mining work and dissatisfied with the upper section of the trail, built a new section which made a "Y" with the trail at the South Rim. In 1879, French married Emma Batchelor, John Doyle Lee's 17th wife. The two moved to Winslow, Arizona, where Emma was known as Dr. French, for her nursing of expectant mothers. (15, 55)

LIPAN POINT: The Lipan Tribe of Apache Indians, allies to the Comanches, lived in Texas. The point was first named Lincoln Point for President Abraham Lincoln, but the name was changed in 1902 by Francois Matthes. BGN 1906. (45)

RR   RM 69.5
BASALT CANYON, CREEK, AND CLIFFS: These are named for the dark basalts of the Cardenas Basalt in the Unkar Group, formed about 1.08 billion years ago. BGN 1906, 1932. (45)

APOLLO TEMPLE: Apollo was the sun of Jupiter and the brother of Diana. He was the god of sun in Roman and Greek mythology. The name was suggested by Francois Matthes in 1902. BGN 1906.

VENUS TEMPLE: Venus was the Roman goddess of beauty and love. She was called Aphrodite in Greek mythology. BGN 1906.

JUPITER TEMPLE: Jupiter was the supreme deity of the Romans. He was called Zeus in Greek mythology. BGN 1906.

JUNO TEMPLE: Juno was wife and sister of Jupiter and called the Queen of Heaven in Roman mythology. She is called Hera by the Greeks. BGN 1906.

CAPE FINAL: After rididng five days to reach this point in 1880, Major Clarence E. Dutton finally had a view of Grand Canyon, thus the name. He described it as the most interesting spot on the Kaibab Plateau. BGN 1906. (45)

OCHOA POINT: Frank Bond named this point for Estevan Ochoa (1831-1888), an Arizona pioneer from Mexico. Ochoa's property was confiscated by Confederate soldiers and he was driven out of Tucson when he refused to swear allegiance to the Confederate cause. But he later returned when the Union troops retook Tucson. He was the mayor of Tucson in 1875 and was a prominent sheep rancher. BGN 1932. (45)

RL   RM 71
CARDENAS CREEK AND BUTTE: These places are named for Garcia Lopez de Cardenas, a lieutenant of Francisco Vasquez de

Coronado, who was dispatched to find the Indian tribe (presumably the Havasupai) who had been described by the Hopi Indians to live near a great river far to the west. Cardenas and his men were guided by the Hopis and reached the South Rim after a 20 day march in September 1540. He and his men are credited to be the first expedition of white men to see the Grand Canyon. The exact localtion where they saw the Grand Canyon is unknown, but Cardenas described it as "elevated and full of low twisted pines, very cold, and lying open to the north." The location is popularly thought to be between Moran Point and Desert View. Bert Loper's bones were washed ashore and found near Cardenas Creek by a hiker in 1975. (45, 54)

HILLTOP RUINS: This Anasazi structure is visible on the crest of the hill. The ruins were discovered by Stanton in 1890, and are thus sometimes called Stanton's Fort. (94)

RR   RM 72.5

UNKAR CREEK AND RAPIDS: Unkar is a Paiute word meaning red creek or red stone. The Anasazi ruins on the delta were excavated under the direction of Douglas Schwartz in the summers of 1967 and 1968. The delta was used seasonally by the Anasazi from 850 to 1200 A.D. A loop trail, less than a mile, will take you on a tour of ten sites. This is one of the largest archeological sites visitors can visit along the river. BGN 1906. (42, 54)

SOLOMON TEMPLE: Solomon, the son of David, was the king of Israel, who reigned for 40 years (973-833 B.C.) and was famous for his wisdom. The temple was named by Francois Matthes. BGN 1906.

SHEBA TEMPLE: The Queen of Sheba journeyed to Israel to test Solomon with hard questions. Sheba is the ancient country in Arabia famous for its trade in spices and gems. Apparently, Sheba and Solomon were more than friends and had a son whose descendants became the ruling emperors of Ethiopia. BGN 1906.

THE TABERNACLE: The tabernacle was the tent used by the Jews as a portable sanctuary before their final settlement in Palestine. It is also an ornamental receptacle for the reserved eucharist, now generally found on the altar. BGN 1906.

FREYA CASTLE: In Scandinavian mythology, Freya was the goddess of fruitfulness and sexual love who also claimed half of those slain in battle. She was the daughter of Njord, the god who dispensed riches and the sister of Freyr, the god who cared for the fruits of the earth. Friday was named in honor of Freya. BGN 1906.

ANGELS WINDOW: Origin unknown. This arch in the Kaibab Limestone at the rim is much photographed and is visible from the Unkar Delta area.

RR   RM 74.5

RATTLESNAKE CAMP: This campsite at 74.5 Mile is unofficially called Rattlesnake Camp by some river guides. Apparently, one dark night, a passenger was using the porta potty and did not have a flashlight. He was bitten by what was described as a black-tailed rattlesnake while reaching for the toilet paper. The Northern Black Tailed Rattlesnake is a nocturnal snake which feeds on rodents and has a distinctive black or dark brown tail. It is rarely found in Grand Canyon, preferring the higher elevations around Flagstaff. The tail of the vermilion to salmon pink colored Grand Canyon Rattlesnake is often dark in color. It is commonly found along the Colorado River. It is mild mannered, often refusing to strike. (136)

RL   RM 75

ESCALANTE CREEK AND BUTTE: Fray Silvestre Velez de Escalante and Fray Francisco Atanasio Dominguez led an expedition from Mexico in 1775-76 to find a practical route between Santa Fe, New Mexico, and Monterrey, California. In 1869, Powell named the creek to honor Escalante, calling it Escalante River. BGN 1906, 1932. (44, 45)

RL   RM 75.5

NEVILLS RAPID AND 75 MILE CREEK: This rapid was named for Norman Davies Nevills (1908-1949), a river runner who began Mexican Hat Expeditions. He built three cataract boats (sometimes called sadirons as they are shaped like old fashioned clothes irons) which he named the *Mexican Hat*, *Botany*, and *WEN* (after his father's initials). Nevills guided the Grand Canyon's first commercial river party in the summer of 1938. Among the passengers where botanists Dr. Elzada Clover and Lois Jotter, the first women to complete a Grand Canyon voyage. On

September 19, 1949, the plane he piloted malfunctioned and crashed, killing both Norm and his wife Doris. BGN 1969. (23, 63, 127)

PAPAGO CREEK: The Papagos are a branch tribe of the Pima Indians of southern Arizona. The name was given by Frank Bond, then Chairman of the BGN. BGN 1932. (45)

> **HOLLENBECK POINT:** John Hance named this point in 1897 for Amelia B. and Josephine W. Hollenbeck, sisters who visited the Grand Canyon in that year. It was renamed Papago Point in 1906, but the original name was restored for the sisters by the BGN in 1985. (127, 128)

> **ZUNI POINT:** The Zuni Indians live in western New Mexico. The Seven Cities of Cibola were thought by the Spanish conquistadores to be in the Zuni lands. BGN 1906.

> **PINAL POINT:** This point was named to honor Pinal County, but it is also a tribal name for the Pinal Apaches. BGN 1906. (45)

RED CANYON: Red Canyon is a descriptive name. The Hance Trail which links the rim to the river was built by John Hance and many other prospectors about 1884, for mining and tourism. Red Canyon was called Dyke Creek by Powell's second expedition in 1872. Dyke is an old spelling for dike, in reference to the near vertically intruded basalt dike in the Hakatai Shale on river right at the head of the rapids. Red Canyon was called Congress Canyon on Charles D. Walcott's 1890s geologic map. BGN 1906. (1, 104, 105)

> **CORONADO BUTTE:** Francisco Vasquez de Coronado was sent by Mendoza, the governor of New Spain, the early name for Mexico, to search for the Seven Cities of Cibola. Fray Marcos de Niza had earlier reported seeing the golden cities from a distance. Coronado set out in 1540 with 366 soldiers and over a hundred others including wives, children, and Indians. In June, he conquered the Zuni city of Hawikuh and after penetrating as far as Kansas returned home sad, weary, and without the golden wealth. BGN 1906. (45, 103)

MORAN POINT: Thomas Moran visited the North Rim with Powell in 1873. Moran's etchings, taken from Beaman's and Hiller's photographs, illustrated Powell's report of his explorations. His landscape paintings and drawings first introduced the American public to the beauty of the Grand Canyon. BGN 1906. (45, 54)

RL/RR   RM 76.5

HANCE RAPIDS: Formed by debris from Red Canyon, this rapid is the biggest river drop in the Grand Canyon (at normal water levels) at 30 feet. It is named for John Hance, sometimes called Captain John Hance, a native of Tennessee, who joined the Confederate Army in the Civil War. He was taken prisoner by the Union Forces and joined their army. After the Civil War, he came to Arizona from Missouri with an ox team, and hauled fodder for Army horses at Camp Verde. He first saw the canyon in 1883 when he was breaking horses for William Hull, who with his brother Phillip, owned a sheep ranch several miles south of the Canyon. The Hulls were the first tourist guides. The first tourist (February 1884) was Edward E. Ayer, a lumberman who started the first lumber company in Flagstaff in 1882. In 1885, Hance took possession of Glendale Spring on the rim and with William Hull, built a log cabin for tourists. Hance then built a trail by improving an old Indian Trail. When tourism was slow, Hance made a few small copper and asbestos discoveries. In his later years, Hance was given lodging by the Fred Harvey Company in the Bright Angel Lodge. He entertained visitors with tall tales until he died in Flagstaff, a pauper, in 1919. He is buried in the Pioneer Cemetery at South Rim. See Hance Creek. BGN 1932. (7, 54, 64, 104)

RM 77 to 118

UPPER GRANITE GORGE: Powell reached the Upper Granite Gorge on August 14, 1869 and wrote in his account, "At daybreak we walk down the bank of the river, on a little sandy beach, to take a view of a new feature in the canyon. Heretofore hard rocks have given us bad river; soft rocks, smooth water; and a series of rocks harder than any we have experienced sets in. The river enters the gneiss! We can see but a little way into the granite gorge, but it looks threatening." BGN 1906, 1925. (83)

The Precambrian rocks are intensely crumpled and mashed due to the mountain-building stress. Molten granite has invaded the schist and gneiss, hence the name. However, Granite Gorge is somewhat of a misnomer as the pink granite comprises only a fraction of the metamorphic rock. Upper Granite Gorge is considered to be 41 miles long, stretching from the bottom of Hance Rapid to below Elves Chasm. (45)

RL   RM 77.5
MINERAL CANYON: This may be named for the abundant alkali which flows down the rock walls, or for the asbestos deposits nearby. BGN 1906.

> **AYER POINT:** This point is named for Emma Burbank Ayer, wife of Flagstaff's first lumberman. She was the first white woman to hike down into the Grand Canyon in May 1885. She, her husband Edward, daughter Elizabeth, and a few others were guided by Bill Hull down the Old Hance Trail. In 1916, Emma translated into English the *Memorial of Fray Alonso de Benavides*, originally written in 1628. (45)

RR   RM 78
ASBESTOS CANYON: John Hance, William Ashurst, John Marshall, and C.H. McClure discovered an asbestos vein here and worked the mine until 1895. The canyon was originally called Salt Creek. Asbestos fibers up to four inches long were mined in the limestone layers of the Bass Formation near the contact zone with the basalt sill. Chlorite, serpentine, and talc are also present. The NPS has placed the mine off-limits to visitation due to the health hazard created by the asbestos. In jest, some river guides say that Hance mined as best as he could. BGN 1906. (45, 54)

> **RAMA SHRINE:** Rama is the Hindu word for prince. It is also the name of the three avatars (or the incarnate form of a deity on earth) of Vishnu and the heroes of Hindu mythology: Balarama, Parashurama, and Ramachandra. BGN 1906.

> **KRISHNA SHRINE:** Krishna is the name of the eighth of the ten incarnations of the supreme god Vishnu in Hindu mythology. Buddha is the ninth; and the tenth is said still to come. BGN 1906.

RL   RM 78.5
HANCE CREEK: John Hance (1838-1919) was a tourist guide, trail-builder, and miner. He supplied visitors to South Rim with log cabin accommodations, meals, and guided tours. When not working his

asbestos mines, he regaled tourists with tall tales for which he became famous. One such tale was that his index finger was shortened, because he plumb wore it off from pointing out all the beautiful scenery to the tourists. Chester Dorland wrote in Hance's guest book, "Captain John Hance -- a genius, a philosopher, and a poet, the possessor of a fund of information vastly important, if true. He laughs with the giddy, yarns to the gullible, talks sense to the sedate, and is the most excellent judge of scenery, human nature and pie. To see the Canyon only, and not to see Captain John Hance, is to miss half the show." BGN 1906. (54, 64, 111)

SOCKDOLAGER RAPIDS: This rapid was named by the men of Powell's second expedition (1871-72). The term is an 1800s U.S. slang for a heavy or knock-down blow, a finisher. According to the Oxford English Dictionary it can also mean something exceptional in any respect, especially a large fish or a form of a fish-hook where two hooks close upon each other by means of a spring as soon as the fish bites. Major Powell called the Grand Canyon below the Little Colorado River the Sock-dologer of the World. BGN 1932. (32, 33, 45)

SINKING SHIP: Then Park Superintendent R. R. Tillotson suggested this name in 1930 due to the tilted strata resembling a sinking ship. It had earlier been known as The Three Castles and is sometimes confused with the Battleship to the west. BGN 1932. (45, 55)

RL   RM 80.5
COTTONWOOD CREEK: This is a descriptive name for the presence of Fremont Cottonwood trees in the drainage above the river. BGN 1932.

HORSESHOE MESA AND CAVES: This is a descriptive name for the shape of the mesa as seen from above. The caves in the Redwall Limestone on the west side take their name from the mesa. BGN 1906, 1937.

GRANDVIEW POINT AND TRAIL: The point was given this descriptive name by John Hance, but it is sometimes called Paiute Point. The trail, first called the Berry Trail but renamed by the NPS, was built by Pete Berry in 1882-1893 to provide access to his copper mines. BGN 1932. (45)

VISHNU CREEK AND TEMPLE: Vishnu was the redeemer or preserver according to the Hindu religion. Vishnu was named by Clarence E. Dutton in 1880, who wrote, "It is a gigantic butte, so admirably designed and so exquisitely decorated that the sight of it must call forth an expression of wonder and delight from the most apathetic beholder." The Creek was originally called Willow Creek in the 1890s. BGN 1906. (45, 36, 130)

WOTANS THRONE: Wotan was the chief deity in German mythology. He is also known as Woden to the Celts and Odin to the Norse. Wednesday is named after Woden. Wotans Throne was named by Francois Matthes and had previously been called Newberry Terrace, a name later given to the butte below. BGN 1906.

NEWBERRY BUTTE: This is named for Dr. John Strong Newberry (1822-1892), the geologist and surgeon who accompanied the Ives expedition of 1857-58. Newberry was the first geologist to study, "the most splendid exposure of stratified rocks that there is in the world." He first propounded the theory that water and the uplift of the continent accounted for the existence of the Grand Canyon. BGN 1906. (55)

CAPE ROYAL: Major Clarence E. Dutton named this headland at the end of the Kaibab in 1882, describing that from this view a "congregation of wonderful structures, countless and vast, the profound lateral chasms, the still lower but unseen depths of the central abyss that holds the river, and the overwhelming palisade of the southern wall" could be viewed. It had previously been called Greenland Point by the Mormon cattlemen. BGN 1906. (36, 45, 47)

HALL BUTTE: Andrew Hall was an 18-year old Scottish lad who joined Powell's first river expedition in 1869. Powell described him as never being "encumbered by unnecessary scruples in giving to his narratives those embellishments which help to make a story complete." He was known to his friends as "Dare-devil Dick." BGN 1932. (5, 45, 83)

GRAPEVINE CREEK AND RAPIDS: This name has been used since the early 1900s. Some say that in low water, the abundance of rocks in the rapid at the mouth of Grapevine Canyon reminded Major Powell's men of a cluster of grapes on the vine, thus the name. Harvey Butchart, famous canyon hiker, suggests that a trickle of water in the Tonto Section which supports a dense stand of wild grapevines is probably the origin of the name. BGN 1906, 1932. (19, 152)

> **LYELL BUTTE:** Sir Charles Lyell (1798-1875) was a British geologist whose ideas, published in *Principles of Geology*, were the direct forerunners of evolutionary theory advanced by Charles Darwin. BGN 1906. (39)

> **SHOSHONE POINT:** The Shoshone Indians lived in northwest Wyoming. The Shoshonean linguistic group (uto-Aztecan) includes that of the Comanche, Ute, Paiute, and Hopi. An earlier name is Cremation Point, named for the local Indian custom of dumping ashes of the dead into the canyon. BGN 1906.

BOULDER CREEK: The creek is so named because the drainage is filled with boulders. BGN 1906. (39)

> **NEWTON BUTTE:** The butte was named for Sir Isaac Newton (1642-1727), a British scientist, mathematician, and philosopher famous for a formulation and proof of the law of gravity. He also devised the binomial theorum and elements of differential calculus. BGN 1906.

83 MILE RAPIDS: This rapid, a ledge at low water, may have been the rapid described by Sumner in his journal on 14 August, 1869, "After running probably another mile we encountered another rapid, or rather a fall -- the only direct fall we encountered on the river. It was a direct straight fall, reaching entirely across the river, with a drop of about eight feet. As we could see no great danger below, I determined to run it, a decision that all agreed to. So out we pulled and made for it full speed, and jumped it like jumping a hurdle with a bucking horse -- and didn't ship enough water to moisten a postage stamp. The fall gave off a peculiar sound at intervals of about ten seconds that sounded precisely like a minute gun at sea. Hence it was called Minute Gun Falls. And so it went -- rapids, daily duckings (sic), and 'heap hungry' all the time." (24)

Clyde Eddy described 83 Mile Rapid as a "short, sharp and vicious drop." Eddy ran the Colorado in 1927 with Nathaniel Galloway's son, Parley, as a guide. The trip included eight college-age, "pink wristed" boys, a dog named Rags, and a bear cub named Cataract. (37)

RL   RM 84
LONETREE CANYON: Two lone Fremont Cottonwood trees were found at a small spring in this drainage. BGN 1932.

> **PATTIE BUTTE:** James Ohio Pattie was a fur trapper and explorer who passed by the Grand Canyon area in 1826 in search of beaver. BGN 1932. (45)

RR   RM 84
CLEAR CREEK: This is a descriptive name for the clear water to be found in the perennial creek. The 1962 Jones roll map calls this Clearwater Canyon. BGN 1906. (152)

> **HAWKINS BUTTE:** William "Billy" Rhodes Hawkins (or Missouri Rhodes) was a mountaineer and Union veteran. He was the cook on Powell's first Grand Canyon trip in 1869. He and Andy Hall rowed the *Kitty Clyde's Sister* and continued down from the Virgin River to the Gulf of California. They thus became, the "first down the Colorado River from Wyoming to Mexico." BGN 1932. (83)

> **DUNN BUTTE:** Frank Bond named this in 1906 for William "Bill" H. Dunn who was on Powell's first river expedition in 1869. He was a mountaineer and trapper. He disappeared along with the Howland brothers after leaving the expedition at Separation Canyon. BGN 1932. (45, 83)

> **THE HOWLANDS BUTTE:** This butte commemorates the Howland brothers Oramel, a Colorado editor, and Seneca, a Union veteran of Gettysburg who separated from the first Powell expedition at Separation Canyon. At first, they rowed the *No Name*, which was destroyed at Disaster Falls in Ladore Canyon, two weeks into the expedition. BGN 1932. (45, 83)

OBI CANYON AND POINT: Obi is Paiute for pinyon pine, or nut pine. The pinyon nut was a major staple or food of Southwestern Indians, providing fat and protein. BGN 1906. (45)

ANGELS GATE: Angels Gate was named by George Wharton James for the place of the descent of the gods of one of the Paiute tribes from the "shadow world above" to the "world of the here" below. The gods would lead the Indian from their present homes of poverty, toil, and ceaseless struggle to their new and blessed homes of plenty, comfort, and rest. South Rim residents often call the formation Snoopy's Dog House as it resembles the profile of Snoopy and his feet as if he was reclining on the roof of his dog house. BGN 1906. (55)

CHEYAVA FALLS: This falls in upper Clear Creek was first noticed by William Beeson in May 1903 who pointed it out to Emery and Ellsworth Kolb, who then visited it. Colonel Birdseye suggested that an Indian word be used, so Ellsworth named it Cheyava, the Hopi word for intermittent, because the falls exist only in the spring with runoff from the North Rim. BGN 1932. (45)

THOR TEMPLE: Thor was the second principal Norse deity and the god of thunder. He was the son of Odin, the supreme being and Jordh, the earth. Thursday is named after Thor. BGN 1906. (90)

HONAN POINT: Honan, or Honani, is the Hopi word meaning badger. The Badger Clan is one of the four most important Hopi clans, along with the Bear, Eagle, and Parrot. The clan originated in South America, is the custodian of the sacred spruce tree, and represents the cardinal direction of north (for that is the direction from which the clan entered Oraibi. BGN 1906. (91, 106)

WALHALLA PLATEAU AND GLADES: Matthes named Walhalla Plateau and Glades. Walhalla (or Valhalla, val means slain and halla means hall) is the great hall of the Scandinavian gods in Asgard, the home of the gods. It was here that Odin received the souls of the slain Viking warriors and heros. Variant names include Valhala Plateau and Valhala Glades, as well as Greenland Plateau and Glades, the Mormon cattleman's name for a nearby spring. BGN 1906. (44)

OTTOMAN AMPHITHEATER: The Ottomans were a Turkish dynasty, noted for opulent magnificence. Founded in 1300, the empire held sway over large dominions in Asia, Africa, and Europe for six centuries until its collapse after World War I. Dutton applied the name in 1882. A variant name is Otoman Zardusht Hanish. BGN 1906. (127)

ARIEL POINT: Francois Matthes named the point. Ariel is the second closest of the four moons of Uranus. In Shakespeare's *Tempest*, Ariel is a spirit of the air who is required to use magic to help Prospero. BGN 1906. (44)

FRANCOIS MATTHES POINT: Francois Emile Matthes (1874-1948), a naturalized American born in Holland, was in charge of making the first topographic maps of Grand Canyon using triangulation, leveling, and plane-table methods. He directed the making of the Vishnu and Bright Angel (1902-1904), Shinumo (1905), and Supai (1920-1921) quadrangles, the later mapped by Richard Evans. Additional areas were mapped in 1923. The maps were made using a 50-foot contour interval at a scale of 1:48,000. In 1902, he and his crew improved a miner's trail down Bright Angel Canyon from the North Rim, later improved by David Rust. Matthes named many of the features in Grand Canyon (Krishna Shrine, Solomon Temple, Woton's Throne, Walhalla Plateau) following Dutton's heroic nomenclature. (45, 70, 90)

RR   RM 84.5

ZOROASTER CANYON AND TEMPLE: Zoroaster (or Zarathustra, 1000 B.C.) was the Persian founder of the ancient religion in the region now known as Iran. Zoroastrianism teaches that there is a continuous struggle between the Good Spirit of the cosmos against the Evil Spirit. George W. James first used the name and it was also applied by Dutton. BGN 1906. (45, 55)

BRAHMA TEMPLE: Brahma was the evolver or the supreme creator of the universe according to the Hindu religion and one of the triad with Vishnu and Shiva. The temple was first named by Clarence E. Dutton, then later submitted to BGN by Matthes. BGN 1906. (45)

DEVA TEMPLE: Deva Temple was first named by Dutton and later submitted to BGN by Henry Gannett. A deva is a god or divinity in the order of good spirits in Hindu mythology. Deva is also the divine epithet applied to the goddess Durga, wife of Shiva. BGN 1906. (90)

DEMARAY POINT: Arthur Edward Demaray (1887-1958) worked for the NPS for 32 years, was the Director of the NPS in 1951, and is buried in the Grand Canyon Pioneer Cemetery. BGN 1964. (44)

BRADLEY POINT: Sergeant George Y. Bradley, a Union veteran of Fredericksburg, was a boatman on Powell's first expedition of 1869, rowing the *Maid of the Canyon.* Powell had asked President Grant to give Bradley a discharge so he could join the expedition. BGN 1932. (45, 83)

SUMNER BUTTE: Jack C. Sumner was a Union veteran, Indian trader, professional guide, and hunter. He was a boatman on Powell's first expedition of 1869, rowing the *Emma Dean,* the flagship named after Powell's wife. BGN 1932. (45, 83)

RL   RM 86
CREMATION CREEK: At the top of this canyon, Indians claimed they used to cremate bodies and throw the ashes off the cliff. BGN 1906. (45)

YAKI POINT: This point was named prior to 1910 for the Yaqui Indians of Mexico by George W. James. Yaqui is a variant spelling. BGN 1906, 1988. (45)

O'NEILL BUTTE: William O. "Bucky" O'Neill (1860-1898), so nicknamed because he was fond of "bucking the tiger" or playing faro, a card game, promoted copper mines and the railroad at Grand Canyon. As Sheriff of Yavapai County in 1889, he pursued and caught train robbers on the mesa above Lee's Ferry. He wrote in John Hance's visitor's book, "God made the canyon, John Hance the trails. Without the other, neither would be complete." He organized the Rough Riders for

the Spanish American War where he was killed on San Juan
Hill. Bucky's cabin, which he used during his gold prospecting
days, is the oldest structure still standing and one of the Bright
Angel Lodge's cabins. BGN 1964. (45, 54, 111)

RL/RR   RM 87.5

KAIBAB SUSPENSION BRIDGE: A swinging bridge was originally
built by the NPS. Started December 15, 1920 and completed May 15,
1921, it had a 420 ft deck span, with 500 ft between bearings and was
supported by two 7/8 inch steel cables. During the winter of 1928, a
second rigid steel suspension bridge was built and is called the "black
bridge" by river runners. It is made with ten 548 ft steel cables, each
1.5 inches in diameter and weighing 2,030 pounds. They were carried
one at a time on the shoulders of a gang 50 (mostly Havasuapai) men
down the South Kaibab Trail. The bridge is 440 ft long, 5 ft wide, and
65 ft above the river. (54)

> **ROYS BEACH:** Royal J. "Roy" Starkey was the resident
> hydrographer at the Bright Angel gage for the USGS. He
> reported the river stage, made measurements, and serviced the
> gage. Overtaken by modern technology in 1977 when an
> automated Data Collection Platform was installed, he was
> reassigned, but returned to Phantom Ranch to work for the Fred
> Harvey Company as a maintenance man. One day, he became
> catatonic over a cup of coffee in the employee's dining room at
> the Ranch. A stroke was suspected and he was flown out to a
> hospital. Roy used to spend time at "his" beach under the
> cableway at river right, where he could lie in the shade of the
> tamarisks, unseen by visitors on the bridge, away from the bustle
> of Phantom Ranch. (137)

> **SOUTH KAIBAB TRAIL:** In 1919, the NPS, unable to buy
> the Bright Angel Trail from Coconino County, constructed the
> South Kaibab or Yaki Trail. (54)

> **THE TIPOFF:** This is the point at which the South Kaibab
> Trail drops almost 1,500 ft from the Tonto Platform to the
> Colorado River.

> **CEDAR RIDGE:** Cedar is the word given to junipers which
> grow with pinyon pine trees on the ridge.

RR   RM 87.5

BRIGHT ANGEL CANYON, CREEK, SPRING, AND FAULT:
Powell stopped here on August 15, 1869, named the creek, and wrote in
his account, "...here is a clear, beautiful creek, or river as it would be
termed in this western country, where streams are not abundant. We
have named one stream, away above, in honor of the great chief of the
Bad Angels, and as this is in beautiful contrast to that, we conclude to
name it Bright Angel." Powell may have been inspired by the name
used by Milton in his 1667 epic poem *Paradise Lost*. The name,
however, was an afterthought. Powell and his men first called it Silver
Creek. Jack Sumner told Robert Stanton that the name came from
chunks of silver "float" ore that they found in the creek while searching
for timber to make oars. The rapid at Bright Angel Canyon is called the
Devil's Spittoon on the 1962 Jones roll map. BGN 1906. (45, 83, 94,
152)

Of course, in 1902, John Hance told a different story: "Yaas, Buckey
O'Neil gave it that name... I'll tell ye how 't was. We never did know
where she come from, ner how she got here, all to once she was here,
and 'peared like she'd come to stay. She was sickly; you could see that,
but she never complained none; was allers just as doggone cheerful as a
sunshiny mornin. Gad! but she was beautiful. She had fluffy hair that
was a streak o' sunlight streamin' through a winder and her skin soft as
velvet, and just white and pink, and she didn't look like a person that
was intended to live on earth; leastwise in no such outlandish place as
this. An' the girl was just as good as she looked, I want t' tell ye. The
boys all fell in love with her; Pete Berry, over at Grand View, an' Bass,
down at the ferry, an' I guess I had a sort o' tender regard fer her
myself. She used t' go down th' trail on every day, walkin' and lookin'
at the' wonderful sights in th' canyon with them blue eyes o' hers, that
was like little patches of th' sky. Boys ust t' watch her, standing on the
rim, till she'd get t'l be nuthin' but a tiny spec o' bright color, movin'
along th' rim. Sometimes there'd be moisture in Buckey's eyes, and I
dunno but mine, too, when we was lookin' at her, and feelin' mabbe she
wasn't goin' t' last long. Buckey ust t' say she was an angel; he knowd
she was, an' he turned out t' be right, fer one day she went down th'
trail an' never came back. There was a sort o' haze like hangin' in th'
canyon that afternoon, an' long about sundown th' light struck it
slanatwise and colored it up like gold. You coun't see fer into th'
canyon, but Buckey claimed he seen somethin' floatin' up through th'

mist, white an' sort of transparient like, but he know'd it was her. There wasn't no doubt about her bein' an angel after that, so he named th' trail "Bright Angel Trail," an' that's how it come. Ye see, Buckey was a sentimental feller, anhow, natcherly, we'd bin a-callin' her th' "Bright Girl," after we found out 'twas Bright's disease that ailed her, so Buckey says, "We'll call it Bright Angel." (123)

Floods down Bright Angel Creek watershed can be catastrophic. A flood of August 1936 was estimated at 4,400 cfs and the flood of December 5-7, 1966 had a flood peak discharge of about 4,000 cfs. This flood caused heavy damage to the newly constructed water pipeline to South Rim and the North Kaibab Trail. A new pipeline was completed in 1970. (26)

> **PHANTOM RANCH AND CREEK:** David Rust worked with his father-in-law "Uncle Dee" or E.D. Woolley of Kanab to build a cable crossing over the Colorado River. He improved Matthes' trail down the Bright Angel Creek, and in 1907 installed the cable tramway 60 feet above the river near the mouth of the creek. Earlier in 1903 he established a camp during trail construction which became a stopping place for travelers and hunting parties, calling it "Rust's Camp." Rust was the first to undertake commercial boating through Glen Canyon for paying passengers, running his trips from 1923 to 1930. BGN 1906. (45, 54, 90)

In 1913, the location was called Roosevelt's Camp, because Theodore Roosevelt stayed there. In 1921-22, the Fred Harvey Company constructed a resort designed by Mary Jane Colter. Colter named Phantom Ranch after Phantom Creek, so named by early surveyors because of the phantom-like haze, an illusory effect of the narrow gorge as seen above in the late afternoon. A swimming pool (filled in with dirt in 1972) and a campground were constructed by the NPS using Civilian Conservation Corps labor in 1935. The CCC boys also planted the cottonwood trees and dug irrigation ditches to keep them alive. Many South Rim visitors may wonder what the Ranch produces or what the mules descending into the canyon may be rounding up. Ask one of the mule wranglers. (45, 54, 90)

NORTH KAIBAB TRAIL: The 14 mile North Kaibab Trail is usually closed from mid-November to mid-May. In 1902, the topographer Francois Matthes and his men on their way back to the South Rim passed two haggard prospectors on their way out. At that time, the route was steep and dangerous. Trail improvements and a suspension bridge across the river have made the trail a main artery for cross canyon travel. (70)

HAUNTED CANYON: Origin unknown. Unfortunately, the following story, often referenced is not correct, for it never happened in Grand Canyon. In 1891, Pete Gann camped in a canyon on the Irion Ranch, in Pinal County. During a dark and stormy night, rolling rocks and stones led him to believe the place was haunted. BGN 1906. (44)

THE BOX: This is a descriptive name for the narrowest part of Bright Angel Creek near the junction with Phantom Creek. BGN 1988. (127)

THE COLONNADE: The descriptive name colonnade refers to a series of columns or arches, set at regular intervals. BGN 1906.

OUTLET CANYON AND SPRING: This is a descriptive name, for this canyon is the main outlet or drainage of The Basin, a valley on the North Rim. BGN 1906. (84)

THE BASIN: This is a descriptive name for the area which functions as the hydrographic basin for the North Rim. BGN 1932. (84)

JONES POINT: Stephen V. Jones was a mathematician and surveyor on Powell's second Grand Canyon expedition (1871-72). The name was suggested by Frank Bond in 1929. BGN 1932. (45)

HATTAN BUTTE: Andy Hattan was the cook on Powell's second expedition. Frank Bond suggested the name in 1929. BGN 1932. (45)

JOHNSON POINT AND STURDEVANT POINT: Glen E. Sturdevant and Fred Johnson, NPS rangers, were killed while trying to cross the Colorado River in their light boat above Horn Creek in 1929. A third member of the group, James P. Brooks, was the sole survivor and was able to hike upstream to Phantom Creek. Glen was the first man specifically hired for summer work as a ranger-naturalist. A graduate of the University of Arizona in geology, he gave campfire lectures and led nature walks. He became the first Park Naturalist in 1927 and began the monthly issues of *Grand Canyon Natures Notes*. Superintendent Tillotson suggested the names in 1930. BGN 1932. (45, 54)

HILLERS BUTTE: John K. "Jack" Hillers, a Utah teamster, joined Powell's second expedition. Nicknamed Jolly Jack, he replaced Sumner (from the first expedition) who was prevented from joining the expedition due to high snow in the Rockies. Hillers also replaced the photographers after E.O. Beaman left during the winter encampment at Kanab and James Fennemore was taken ill at Lee's Ferry. Hillers became one of the great photographers of the American West and served as Chief Photographer for the USGS. It is from many of his photographs that Thomas Moran drew his sketches of Grand Canyon which illustrate Powell's report of his explorations. BGN 1932. (45)

CLEMENT POWELL BUTTE: Walter Clement "Clem" Powell is not to be confused with Walter Henry Powell of the first expedition. Clem was Powell's orphaned first cousin. He was 21 years old when he went on Powell's second expedition in 1871-1872 to assist the trip photographer, E.O. Beaman. Beaman departed and because Powell felt that Clem was inept as a cameraman, James Fennemore was hired. But Fennemore became sick and his duties were assumed by Jack Hillers. BGN 1932. (45, 54)

RIBBON FALL: This fall is about one-third the way up the trail to the North Rim. Water spills over a travertine overhang in ribbons, or so thought Francois Matthes who suggested the name. BGN 1906. (45)

KOMO POINT: This is the name of an Indian family and a plant which is used to make a pink dye. It was earlier called Fafner Point. BGN 1906. (127)

WALL CREEK: The NPS named this in 1926. Almon Thompson had named it Beaver Creek, from the Paiute name Pouncagunt meaning beaver in 1872. (1)

MANZANITA CREEK AND POINT: Colonel John White who lived at the Grand Canyon in the 1920s named these features using the Spanish word meaning "little apple" for the two species of Manzanita bushes which grow in the area: Green Leaf Manzanita and Pointleaf Manzanita. BGN 1932. (45)

ROARING SPRINGS AND CANYON: These springs erupt from near the junction of Bright Angel and Roaring Springs Canyons with a roaring sound, hence the name. BGN 1906, 1932. (45)

UNCLE JIM POINT: James T. "Uncle Jim" Owens was appointed warden by the Forest Service for the Grand Canyon Game Reserve which was set aside in 1906. He had a cabin near the rim. The management philosophy of the time was to protect the grazers by killing off the predatory animals such as mountain lions, coyotes, bobcats, owls, hawks, and eagles. Uncle Jim is credited with 532 lion kills. The NPS suggested the name in 1930, Variant names include Lucifer Point and Natchi Point. BGN 1906. (45, 54, 127)

THE TRANSEPT: In 1882, Clarence Dutton named this canyon and said it was "one of the finest and perhaps the most picturesque of the gorges in the whole Kaibab front ... far grander than Yosemite." The transept is said to cross Bright Angel Canyon below its nave. BGN 1906. (45)

THOMPSON CANYON: This canyon and associated spring are named after Thompson, a Mormon cattleman who grazed cattle here with Van Slack using the V.T. brand. BGN 1932. (45)

OZA BUTTE: Oza is a Paiute name for a basket with a bottleneck opening. BGN 1906. (44, 127)

WIDFORSS POINT: Gunnar Mauritz Widforss (1879-1934) was born in Sweden and died at the Grand Canyon. He made many splendid paintings and watercolors of the canyon. Earlier, it had been known as McKinnon Point. In 1892, Colonel H. McKinnon, an English visitor, came here after killing his first buck on the Kaibab with W.S. "Buffalo Bill" Cody. He left a note announcing the event in a tin can at the point. BGN 1937. (45)

MANU TEMPLE: Manu, a Sanskrit word meaning man, is one of the fourteen demiurgic beings or subordinate gods, each of whom presided over a period of race progressions. Manu Vaivasvata, the sun-born, is the manu of the present race of beings. George W. James wrote, "This I have named Manu Temple, after the great law-giver of the Hindoos." BGN 1906. (45, 55)

BUDDHA TEMPLE: The name Buddha Temple was suggested by Henry Gannett, in 1906. Gannet was the geographer for Dutton's survey and later became chief geographer of the USGS. Buddha is the ninth of the ten incarnations of the supreme god Vishnu in Hindu mythology. Buddha was also the title of Siddhartha, the founder of Buddhism in the fifth century B.C. BGN 1906. (45)

NORTH RIM: The North Rim reaches altitudes as high as 8,800 ft. A concessionaire from Yellowstone, W.W. Wylie, opened the first tourist stop in 1917, calling it the Wylie Way Camp. The Grand Canyon Lodge was built in 1928, but later burned down in 1932 and was rebuilt in 1936. About 390,000 people visited North Rim in 1991. BGN 1950. (54, 102)

DE MOTTE PARK: This open meadow on the North Rim was named by Powell in August 1872 for Dr. Harvey Clelland de Motte, a professor of mathematics at Wesleyan University in Illinois. De Motte accompanied Powell on his survey of the North Rim. The area had also been called V.T. Park and V.T. Park Tourist Ranch by the early cattlemen. VT was the brand of the cattle run by Van Slack and Thompson, two Mormon ranchers from Orderville, Utah, who also owned the Valley Tannery. The range was abandoned in 1919 with the establishment of Grand Canyon National Park. BGN 1926. (4, 45)

BRIGHT ANGEL SUSPENSION BRIDGE: This foot bridge was built in 1970 to hold a water pipeline. Water flows from Roaring Springs below the North Rim by gravity to Indian Garden, where it is pumped to the South Rim. (54)

PIPE CREEK: In 1894, Ralph and Niles Cameron, Pete Berry, and James McClure were traveling on the Tonto Trail between Grandview Trail and Bright Angel Trail. Ralph found a Meerschaum pipe on the ground and scratched a date about 100 years previous on it. To complete the joke, he placed it where it could be found by the others who marveled about the early visitor, until Ralph confessed. The stream, which reaches the river, has since been called Pipe Creek. BGN 1932. (45)

> **BRIGHT ANGEL TRAIL:** The Bright Angel Trail was originally called the Cameron Trail. It was constructed in 1891 following an old Indian route by Ralph H. Cameron, Pete Berry, Robert Ferguson, James McClure, and Niles J. Cameron to provide access to their mines. Conflict over ownership arose in 1901. After much legal battling between Cameron, Coconino County, and the railroad, it was sold by Coconino County to the Federal Government in 1928. (104)

> **INDIAN GARDEN:** Havasupai Indians cultivated this area for crops until the early 1900s. But it was a dangerous place to farm as visiting Yavapai and Southern Paiute Indians using the cross canyon trail would help themselves to the harvest. BGN 1932, 1988. (45, 128)

> **GARDEN CREEK:** The water from Garden Creek was used to irrigated the crops at Indian Garden, hence the name. BGN 1906. (45)

> **PLATEAU POINT:** Plateau Point, at approximately 3,780 ft elevation, is reached by trail from Indian Garden and provides an overlook of the Granite Gorge and the Colorado River, about 1,380 ft below. It is easily seen from the South Rim. The point was known as Turtle Head in the 1920s. A World War I flyer, R.V. Thomas, made two landings here in 1922 as part of a publicity stunt. BGN 1932. (54)

THE BATTLESHIP: The ridge looks like an old-style battleship. Emery Kolb called this the Battleship Iowa in 1914, but the name was shortened. BGN 1932. (44)

YAVAPAI POINT: Yavapai Indians, formerly referred to as the Apache-Mohave Indians, are a branch of the Yuman family who lived along the Verde River. The word comes from enyaeva for sun and pai for people. A variant name is O'Neill Point. BGN 1906. (45)

GRANDEUR POINT: A descriptive name. BGN 1932.

MARICOPA POINT: Maricopa Indians lived in south central Arizona. This Yuman tribe lived by the Gulf of California according to Fray Garces in 1775 and had moved north to the mouth of the Gila River by 1826. They lived with the Pima Indians and were noted for being friendly towards white men. A variant name is Sentinel Point. BGN 1906. (45)

The formation at the end of Maricopa Point is sometimes called The Maiden's Breast. George Wharton James reported that the Havasupais gave the name for the fact that "a small nipple in red sandstone" crowns the formation. (55)

MATHER POINT: Stephen Tyng Mather (1867-1930) was the first Director of the NPS when it became an agency in 1916 and served until 1929. Mather was a conservationist and established the policies which defined the Park Service. He had made a fortune in the borax business and paid for many of the badly needed improvements in the early parks. (54)

SOUTH RIM: Located on the south side of the river, the South Rim reaches altitudes up to 7,500 ft. The Grand Canyon Village is the main park administration area and a tourist attraction. Over 4.2 million people visited the Grand Canyon in 1991, over 3.3 million on South Rim and Desert View alone. (54)

RL   RM 90.5
HORN CREEK AND RAPIDS: While the twin waves at the top of Horn Creek Rapid resemble horns, the creek is named after Tom Horn (1860-1903). He was a hero to some and an assassin to others. He is best known as the army scout and Apache interpreter for Al Sieber in his

negotiations with Geronimo. Geronimo, speaking in Apache, told Horn that he spoke very fast and wondered if he could interpret as fast as he talked. Horn replied that Geronimo had but one mouth and tongue that he could see and for him to let loose. Horn later described Geronimo as the biggest chief, the best talker, and the biggest liar in the world. Horn also served under the Generals Willcox, Crook, and Miles. (44, 53)

Horn led a checkered life. He was a swashbuckling adventurer; one of the founding fathers of Tombstone, Arizona; fluent in German, Spanish, and Apache languages; a stage driver; a cowboy (he won the World's Championship at Phoenix in 1891); a miner; a deputy for Sheriff Bucky O'Neill of Yavapai County and for Sheriff Reynolds of Gila County; a rancher; a civilian chief packer in Cuba during the Spanish-American War (he gave Theodore Roosevelt a mule to ride when he discovered Roosevelt afoot during battle); a detective for the Pinkerton National Detective Agency in Denver; and a cattle detective in Wyoming. Sadly, Horn was convicted of murdering 13 year old Willie Nickell and was the first man to be hung in the Wyoming gallows. Henry Gannet suggested the name. BGN 1906. (44, 53)

> **POWELL POINT:** Here, a monument to John Wesley Powell commemorates his achievements as leader of one of the four great surveys of the American West (the others being the Hayden, King, and Wheeler surveys). BGN 1937. (5, 45)

> **HOPI POINT AND WALL:** These features are named for the Hopi Indians, the descendants of the pueblo peoples and the Sinaqua Indians. The word Hopi comes from their word Hopitu, meaning Peaceful Ones, the name the Hopis give themselves. Their reservation, completely surrounded by the Navajo Reservation, was created in 1882. The Hopis reside in seven principle villages. Oraibi, along with Acoma, New Mexico, is the oldest continuously inhabited town in the United States (since 1150 A.D.). Variant names include Rowes and Rowes Point after Sanford Rowe, a pioneer stockman, miner, and guide who built a well and an auto camp close to the rim. BGN 1906. (45)

> **DANA BUTTE:** This butte can be see upstream from Granite Rapids. It was named by George W. James for James Dwight Dana (1813-1895) who was an eminent professor of geology at Yale University for many years. BGN 1906. (45)

SCHELLBACK BUTTE: Dr. Louis Schellback first came to Grand Canyon to work for the NPS in 1933 and served as the Chief Park Naturalist from 1941-1957. BGN 1975.

RR   RM 91.5

TRINITY CREEK: The Trinity is the union of three persons (Father, Son, and Holy Ghost) in one Godhead, or the threefold personality of one Divine Being. BGN 1906.

SHIVA TEMPLE: Clarence E. Dutton named Shiva Temple in 1880 and stated, "All around it are side gorges sunk to a depth nearly as profound as that of the main channel. It stands in the midst of a great throng of cloister-like buttes, with the same noble profiles and strong lineaments as those immediately before us, with a plexus of awful chasms between. In such a stupendous scene of wreck it seems as if the fabled 'Destroyer' might find an abode not wholly uncongenial." Shiva (or Siva) was the destroyer according to the Hindu religion. This avenging associate of Brahma and Vishnu is considered to be the most popular Hindu god. BGN 1906. (45)

The six square miles of forested area on top of Shiva Temple interested biologists. Set apart from the North Rim by thousands of years or more of erosion, it possibly contained plants and animals which had evolved into new species or were unknown to man. To discover these freaks of evolution, the American Museum of Natural History organized a 1937 scientific expedition heralded by the press. After much investment, planning, a parachute drop of supplies, and scaling of its walls, the party mounted the summit. There they found a recently shed pair of deer antlers and a piece of yellow trash -- a cardboard box with the words "Eastman Kodak Panchromatic" written on the side. Obviously, animals had no problem ascending and descending Shiva and the canyon's resident photographer, Emery Kolb, who had not been included in the expedition's plans, had beat the expedition to the punch. Emery told Harvey Butchart that he had climbed Shiva twice, once with his daughter Edith. (54, 131)

CHEOPS PYRAMID: Cheops was an Egyptian pharaoh of the fourth dynasty and builder of the famous Great Pyramid at Gizeh, the oldest of the seven wonders of the ancient world.

The name may have been bestowed by George W. James. BGN 1906. (45)

ISIS TEMPLE: Isis was the principal female deity of Egyptian mythology. She was the wife of Osiris, mother of Horus, and sometimes called "The Daughter of Ra." BGN 1906. (45)

HORUS TEMPLE: Horus in Egyptian mythology was the son of Osiris and Isis. BGN 1906. (90)

OSIRIS TEMPLE: Osiris was the chief Egyptian deity, judge of the dead, ruler of the Kingdom of Ghosts, god of the Nile River, and brother and husband of Isis. His brother Seth murdered him and cut him into 14 pieces, which where reclaimed by Isis. He is linked with resurrection and the afterlife. BGN 1906. (90)

TOWER OF RA: Ra, the Sun God, was the supreme deity of Egyptian mythology who was always victorious. BGN 1906. (45)

TOWER OF SET: Set, the Egyptian god of war, was the brother or son of Osiris and his deadly enemy according to Egyptian mythology. It was named in 1879 by the artist, Thomas Moran. BGN 1906. (45)

TIYO POINT: The Hopi Indians tell the story of Tiyo who journeyed down the Colorado River through Grand Canyon in a cottonwood log to find out where the river went. The journey was a voyage through the Underworld where Tiyo encounters sacred forces and beings that sustain all life. Tiyo met and married a snake girl and their children became the Snake Clan of Walpi. Thus, the legend of Tiyo became an explanation for the origins of the Snake Dance. It had earlier been called Jupiter Point. BGN 1906. (106)

RL   RM 92.5
SALT CREEK: Henry Gannet, Dutton's geographer, named this creek in 1906 for the salty taste of the water. BGN 1906.

THE INFERNO: This is a descriptive name first used on the 1906 Bright Angel quadrangle map. The hellish heat rising from the black, granite walls impressed the early topographers. Francois Matthes reported that the triangulation line had to be run in midsummer, during an unusually hot spell of weather when the lowest temperature recorded was 96 degrees F, at six in the morning. The level bubble would grow smaller and smaller, until by noon it would vanish and work had to be stopped. Also, the levelman could not stand still as he had to lift his feet in alternation, so not to burn them on the hobnails in his shoes. (70)

MOHAVE POINT: The Mohave Indians lived along the lower Colorado River. BGN 1906. (45)

THE ALLIGATOR: This is a descriptive name for the low-lying ridge. BGN 1932. (45)

RL   RM 93.5
MONUMENT CREEK: A descriptive name for the hundred foot high pinnacle in the canyon's floor or bed about one mile up from the Colorado River. BGN 1906. (45)

> **GRANITE RAPIDS:** This rapid, formed by the tributary outwash of Monument Creek, is located in the Granite Gorge of the Colorado River, thus the name. The pink granite in the area is termed the Zoroaster Granite. Variant names include Granite Falls and Monument Creek Rapids. BGN 1932.

> **FOREVER EDDY:** This eddy below Granite Rapids on river right is called "Forever Eddy" by river runners. The eddy fence between the rapid and the eddy is very strong. When the river turns red with sediment from tributary flash floods, the eddy can remain emerald green for some time. Perhaps the earliest account of getting stuck in Forever Eddy is that of Norman Nevills. He wrote, "In '38, after looking over the famous GRANITE FALLS RAPID I elected to run it, and as always ran it first in my boat. At the bottom of the rapids I would bail my boat then signal the next boat to come thru, with my boat in readiness to help if necessary. This program is varied sometimes when I will run all three boats thru. At any rate, this rapid has waves in the main channel which we always run some twenty feet high. These waves ran right alongside the towering right hand wall. I was up on the third tremendous wave when, in

76

going to pull on my left hand oar the oar slipped thru the ring. This immediately caused the boat to slide off the right hand wave and, in turning around end for end dash to the wall at twenty miles an hour! I stood up to fend off as best I could, but fortunately a little side current stopped the boat a foot from the wall! In trying to fend off I cut my knuckles almost to the bone. The oar on the wall side had flipped round and pinned me against the bow splashboard. I extricated myself and found I was in a cove with the big waved river dashing at what seemed lightning-like speed. Finally, with a prayer, I maneuvered the boat out into the current and held out far enough to keep from being redashed into a projection of granite below. Was in the cove like hole for 4 1/2 minutes." (76)

THE ABYSS: This is a descriptive name. BGN 1932. (4, 45)

GREAT MOHAVE WALL: This is named for the Mohave Indians who lived along the Colorado River near Needles. The word mohave means three mountains. The Needles was the name given by Lt. Amiel Whipple for these three sharp peaks in the area. BGN 1932. (45)

COPE BUTTE: Edward Drinker Cope (1840-1897), a noted American vertebrate paleontologist, investigated the Cretaceous and Tertiary strata of the West in the 1870s. BGN 1906. (45)

HERMIT CREEK, RAPIDS, AND FAULT: Hermit Creek is named for Louis Boucher, a quiet man who was called a hermit because he lived in a remote area near Dripping Springs at the head of Hermit Canyon, where he had two tents, a corral for horses, mules, burros, and sheep, and kept goldfish in a trough. He had a second home in Boucher Creek. In the 1910s, the Santa Fe Railroad company improved the trail into the canyon, built a tent village on the Tonto Platform with piped water, and brought in supplies using an aerial tram down from Pima Point. The camp was used until the 1930s. BGN 1906, 1932. (45, 54)

PIMA POINT: The Pima Indians in south central Arizona are a peaceful, agrarian tribe. The name Pima was given by the Spaniards as the tribe used the word pim meaning no. In the early 1900s, it was sometimes called Hermit Point, Seri Point (for a tribe who live in the Gulf of California in Mexico), and

Cyclorama Point. A cyclorama is a pictorial representation, in natural perspective, of a landscape which is painted on the inner wall of a cylindrical room where spectators view it from the center of the room. BGN 1906. (45)

CATHEDRAL STAIRS: The Hermit Trail through the Redwall Limestone is called the Cathedral Stairs as it resembles the tightly wound staircases found in great churches.

LOOKOUT POINT: This is a descriptive name used on a 1906 USGS map. BGN 1932. (45)

BREEZY POINT: Emery and Ellsworth Kolb named this point as the breezes are strong enough to blow gravel. BGN 1932. (45)

COLUMBUS POINT: Christopher Columbus (1446-1506) was the Italian navigator in Spanish service who discovered the Americas in 1492. BGN 1932.

DRIPPING SPRINGS: Louis Boucher named this spring and Henry Gannett, chief geographer of the USGS, submitted the name to the BGN in 1906. (44, 54)

WALDRON TRAIL: Origin unknown.

EREMITA MESA: Eremita (the gender agrees with mesa) is the Spanish word for hermit, in reference to Louis Boucher, the hermit. BGN 1932.

YUMA POINT: The Yuma Indians lived along the lower Colorado River. The name comes from the Spanish word umo, meaning smoke. This is derived from the habit of the tribe of making huge, smokey fires to induce rain. BGN 1906. (45)

RL   RM 95.5
TRAVERTINE CANYON: This name was suggested by geologist Edwin D. McKee for the great quantities of travertine at the Tonto Plateau level. Travertine is a form of limestone or calcium carbonate deposited by springs. Another Travertine Canyon is located at River Mile 229. BGN 1932. (45, 127)

COCOPA POINT: The Cocopah (spelled Cocopa by BGN) Indians lived along the Colorado River below Yuma. A variant spelling is Cocopah. BGN 1906. (45, 127)

WHITES BUTTE: James B. White (1837-1927) is the prospector who claimed to have been the first to descend the Colorado River through Grand Canyon. He said he floated the river in 14 days on a cottonwood log raft in 1867. He was separated from his two prospecting friends after Indians attacked them, killing one partner. The other partner drowned after five days and White continued on a smaller raft. His half-dead body was pulled from the river below Pearce Ferry at Callville, Nevada. Many historians dispute his claim. (21, 45)

RL   RM 96.5
BOUCHER CREEK, TRAIL, AND RAPIDS: Louis D. Boucher, born in Quebec, Canada, arrived in Grand Canyon in 1891. For a while he was a trail guide at Hance Ranch. He later established a tourist camp at his home at Dripping Springs in Hermit Canyon. He constructed the last trail into the canyon (1902-1905), which he called the Silver Bell Trail, perhaps for the bell which hung around the neck of his white mule, Calamity Jane. It is now called the Boucher Trail and links Hermit Canyon with Boucher Creek, where Boucher had a second camp next to a 75 tree orchard of oranges, figs, peaches, and pomegranates and his copper mine. He moved to Utah in 1912 to mine coal. Edwin Corle said of Boucher, "He wore a white beard, rode a white mule, and told only white lies." A variant name is Long Creek or Canyon. BGN 1932. (45, 54, 56)

TOPAZ CANYON: Topaz is a semi-precious stone. BGN 1908. (45)

VESTA TEMPLE: Vesta is the Roman goddess of the hearth in whose honor the Vestal Virgins kept a symbolic fire burning. BGN 1908. (45)

DIANA TEMPLE: Diana is the Roman goddess of the moon and hunting, as well as the protectress of women. The locality was known as No Man's Land in the 1900s. BGN 1908. (44)

MARSH BUTTE: This was named by George Wharton James for Othniel Charles Marsh (1831-1899), an American paleontologist, who discovered the fossilized early ancestors of horses in America. He was in charge of vertebrate paleontology for the USGS for many years. It was earlier called Endymion Dome, after the beautiful Greek youth whom Selene, the goddess of the Moon, caressed as he slept. BGN 1906. (45, 51)

MIMBRENO POINT: Mimbreno is Spanish for willow twigs. The Mimbreno Apache, sometimes called the Mimbres culture, lived in southwestern New Mexico and southeastern Arizona around 1100-1200. BGN 1908. (45)

MESCALERO POINT: The Mescalero Apaches live in New Mexico. BGN 1908. (45)

RR   RM 98

CRYSTAL CREEK AND RAPIDS: Crystal is a descriptive name for the crystal clear water of the stream. An earlier name was West Fork. In 1890, Robert Stanton named this drainage, McDonald Creek, for Harry McDonald who separated from his expedition at this point and hiked out to the North Rim. BGN 1906, 1932. (45)

The catastrophic flood of December 1966 down Crystal Creek transported debris and boulders in excess of five ft in diameter to the Colorado River. The peak discharge was estimated at 29,000 cfs, with most of the flow ranging between 9,200 to 14,000 cfs. This once mild rapid was turned into one of the biggest on the river due to the constriction caused by the tributary debris. High flows of 1983 enlarged the constriction somewhat, but scientists theorize that Colorado River flows of 300,000 to 400,000 cfs are necessary to contour the channel to the pre-1966 shape. (26)

Following Crystal Rapids are several rapids named for gems: Agate, Sapphire, Turquoise, Emerald, Ruby, and Serpentine. Many river guides use the acronyms CASTERS, TASTERS, or ASTER to remember the sequence of these rapids that come in rapid succession.

CLAUDE BIRDSEYE POINT: Colonel Claude Hale Birdseye (1878-1941) was the Chief Topographic Engineer of the USGS, a distinguished soldier in World War I, an eminent photogrammetrist, and leader of the USGS 1923 surveying expedition from Lee's Ferry to Needles. Birdseye is also noted for mapping the volcanos Kilauea and Mount Rainier. BGN 1965. (63, 89)

CONFUCIUS TEMPLE: Confucius (551-478 B.C.) was the Chinese sage and philosopher who taught practical morality: treating others as you wish to be treated, loyalty, intelligence and full developments of the individual in the various relationships in life. A variant combined name for Confucius and Mencius Temples is Twin Butte. BGN 1906. (45)

MENCIUS TEMPLE: Mencius is a name for the Confucian Chinese philosopher Meng-tse (372-289 B.C.). BGN 1906. (90)

DRAGON, HEAD, CREEK AND LITTLE DRAGON: These are descriptive names for the geologic formations which resemble a sleeping dragon. The tail separates the body from the North Rim, the east ridge of the mesa is the backbone, and the head rises to a pyramid-shaped butte at 7,764 ft. The mesa actually seems to breath fire, as it is the site of many wild fires due to its fire load which is higher than any other site. Dragon Head used to be called Holmes Tower after William Henry Holmes who sketched the nearly perfect geologic drawings in Dutton's report. BGN 1906. (55, 84)

MILK CREEK: In 1882, Clarence Dutton named the spring above on the Kaibab Plateau, Milk Spring after the water which has "a faint whitish cast, like that which would be produced by putting a drop or two of milk into a bucket of pure water ... caused by a fine precipitate of lime." BGN 1932. (36)

GRAMA POINT: Blue grama (<u>Bouteloua</u> <u>gracilis</u>) is a native grass which grows at Grama Point and other places on the North Rim in pinyon-juniper and ponderosa pine forests. It is an excellent forage grass and withstands grazing well, tending to increase under heavy grazing. BGN 1906.

HINDU AMPHITHEATER: Major Clarence E. Dutton named this feature in 1882 and wrote that, "The architectural details are always striking, and by their profusion and richness suggest an Oriental character." BGN 1906. (36)

SLATE CREEK AND FAULT: This descriptive name was submitted by the NPS as it was in local usage. The schist and quartzite rocks fracture in a slate-like manner. Slate, a form of metamorphosed shale, is a bluish-gray rock that splits easily into thin, smooth layers. BGN 1932.

> **SCYLLA BUTTE:** Scylla, a lovely nymph, was loved by Glaucus, a fisherman who was made into a sea-god. Circe was enamored of Glaucus and jealously changed Scylla into a frightful monster rooted to a promontory by the sea. Scylla in her misery destroyed everything that came within her reach. Today, Scylla is the name of the dangerous rock on the Italian side of the Strait of Messina, facing Charybdis, a whirlpool on the Sicilian side. Jason, the Argonauts, Aeneas, and Odysseus were tested when sailing by Scylla. The butte had earlier been called Yucatan Temple by George W. James. BGN 1908. (51, 90)

> **GEIKIE PEAK:** Sir Archibald Geikie (1835-1924), the Scottish geologist, was the director-general of the Geological Survey for the United Kingdom and studied the volcanic deposits in Grand Canyon. BGN 1908. (4, 45)

TUNA CREEK AND RAPIDS: Tuna is the Mexican word for any of the various prickly pears of the genus Opuntia or for the sweet, edible fruit of the prickly pear. It had earlier been called Boulder Creek, but was changed to Border Creek by the USGS in 1906, then to Tuna Creek the same year. However, my husband claims that Powell called the canyon star-kissed as he found meteorites embedded in the canyon's floor. BGN 1906.

> **CHARBYDIS BUTTE:** Charybdis was personified in classical mythology as a female monster, who barked like a dog. It is also a boat destroying whirlpool on the Sicilian side of the Strait of Messina, opposite Scylla, a dangerous rock on the Italian side. The phrase, "to be between Charybdis and Scylla," means to be between two evils or dangers, either one of which can be safely avoided only by risking the other. BGN 1908. (51)

POINT SUBLIME: This 7,464 ft point was named by Major Clarence Dutton in 1880. He spent much time here writing of the Grand Canyon scenery. It is reported that he called it, "the most sublime of the earthly spectacles." BGN 1906, 1988. (36, 45)

WALLA VALLEY: The Hopi word wala means either gap or the action of something sloshing or making a wave. Waala, another similar Hopi word, means arroyo, wash, gorge, or ravine. Wala Valley was known as Tranquil Valley and Pond Canyon in the early 1900s. BGN 1964. (44, 91, 127)

RM 99.5

WILLIES NECKTIE OR ESMERALDAS ELBOW RAPIDS: This rapid is named for Wilson "Willie" Taylor, who was a member of Hudson's 1950 inboard motor boat trip on the *Esmeralda II*. Willie fell off the boat and during the rescue two ropes wrapped around his neck. He almost drowned when Otis "Dock" Marston, unaware of his plight, powered upstream dragging him underwater. The *Esmeralda II* was wrecked, left behind, and salvaged the next month by Jim Rigg and Frank Wright. See Willie's Canyon. (63, 133)

RC   RM 100

100 MILE ROCK: This rock in mid-channel is 100 miles below Lee's Ferry. In 1972, river guide Mike Castelli called it Nixon Rock after President Nixon, as he considered it a major obstruction. River guides have played on the name by explaining that the rock is so named as it is a tricky rock just right of center. Additionally, the little rocks just behind Nixon Rock are sometimes called the Spiro Agnew Rocks for the Vice President who seemed to hide in the shadow of the President.

RL   RM 100.5

AGATE CANYON AND RAPIDS: In 1903, Richard T. Evans of the USGS named this canyon for the semi-precious stones found in the canyon. Agate is a variety of quartz with variously colored strips or clouded colors. BGN 1908. (4, 45)

RL   RM 101

SAPPHIRE CANYON AND RAPIDS: Powell named this canyon for its coloring, a feature which can not be seen from the river. Sapphire is a bright blue precious stone that is hard and clear, like a diamond. BGN 1908. (45)

PIUTE POINT: First called Grandview Point, the name was changed to honor the Paiute Indians of the North Rim. A variant spelling is Paiute. BGN 1908. (45)

POLLUX TEMPLE: Pollux was the divine son of Leda and Zeus. He was full brother to Helen of Troy and half-brother to Castor. Pollux and Castor went on the Quest of the Golden Fleece and rescued Helen after Theseus carried her off. Castor was killed over a dispute about oxen and Pollux was inconsolable. Zeus took pity and allowed both to share life, one day in Hades, the next in Olympus, always together. The constellation Gemini represents the brothers. (51, 90)

CASTOR TEMPLE: Castor was the mortal son of Leda and King Tyndareus of Sparta and half-brother to Pollux. A variant name is Castle Temple. BGN 1964. (51)

JICARILLA POINT: The Jicarilla Apache tribe live in New Mexico. They were so-named by the Spaniards as they made xicarillas, or little baskets. BGN 1908. (90)

RL   RM 102

TURQUOISE CANYON AND RAPIDS: Major Powell named this canyon for its coloring. Turquoise is a sky-blue or greenish-blue precious stone. BGN 1908. (45)

SHALER PLATEAU: Nathaniel Southgate Shaler (1841-1906), noted geologist, is called the founding father of American academic geography. He was also one of America's first scientists to advocate the evolutionary ideas of Darwin. A gifted teacher, he taught at Harvard University for 23 years. BGN 1908. (90)

RR   RM 104

EMERALD CANYON: It is not known who named this canyon, but it is named for the bright, transparent green precious stone. Both emeralds and aquamarines are beryls, very hard minerals which are silicates of beryllium and aluminum.

SCORPION RIDGE: A descriptive term for the shape of the ridge as seen from above, Scorpio is the Latin word for scorpion, the eighth sign of the zodiac, and a constellation. BGN 1908. (90)

MONADNOCK AMPHITHEATER: A monadnock is a physical geological term for a residual hill or mountain standing well above the surface of a surrounding peneplain, or a plane leveled by erosion. When the Tonto Sea came in from the west about 570 million years ago, it encountered Precambrian "islands" or hills of Shinumo Quartzite in this area. The term is also a northeastern American Indian term meaning prominent mountain. Mount Monadnock is an isolated peak in New Hampshire at 3,186 ft. BGN 1910. (130)

SAGITTARIUS RIDGE: Sagittarius, the Latin word for archer, is the ninth sign of the zodiac and a constellation representing a centaur drawing a bow. This name for the ridge may be derived as it is eithger stright as an arrow or somewhat curved as a bow. BGN 1908. (90)

EVANS BUTTE: Richard T. Evans worked on the topography of the Shinumo (1905) and Vishnu (1907) quadrangles with Francois Matthes, then completed other USGS topographic maps in Grand Canyon from 1920-1923. He named many features. BGN 1969. (70)

RL   RM 104.5
RUBY CANYON AND RAPIDS: It is not known who named this canyon after the clear, hard red, precious stone. BGN 1908.

WALAPAI POINT: This is not the usual spelling for the Hualapai Indians who are honored by this point. Hualapai means people of the tall pines. The Hualapai Indian Reservation borders the Grand Canyon. BGN 1932. (90)

LE CONTE PLATEAU: Joseph Le Conte took observations with a stationary barometer for Dr. Arnold Guyot, who explored this locality and proposed the name. Le Conte was also a professor of geology for thirty years at the University of California. BGN 1908. (45)

SERPENTINE CANYON AND RAPIDS: William W. Bass named this canyon. Serpentine is an altered peridotite and pyroxenite. Serpentine is a group of minerals produced by contact metamorphism, or heat and pressure alternation, between the basalt sills in contact with the Bass Limestone. Serpentine can also mean like a serpent, winding and twisting, or cunning, sly, or treacherous. BGN 1908, 1932. (55)

> **GRAND SCENIC DIVIDE:** This ridge was named by William W. Bass, as it divides the Tonto Platform to the east and the Esplanade to the west. A tower, called Dick Pillar, at the end of the ridge honors Robert Dick of Thurso, Scotland, who studied sandstone. BGN 1932. (45, 55)

> **HAVASUPAI POINT:** The Havasupai Indians live in Havasu Creek, in the Grand Canyon. See Havasu Canyon. BGN 1932. (45)

BASS CANYON, RAPIDS, TRAIL, AND CAMP: William Wallace Bass (1841-1933) established a camp in the late 1880's on the South Rim. He constructed the Mystic Springs Trail to the Colorado River (later called the Bass Trail) and in 1908 built a cable-car crossing across the river to his asbestos and copper mines on the north side. He lived on the South Rim with his wife Ada Diefendorf Bass and their four children. By 1902, Bass guided tourist, prospecting, and hunting parties in the canyon, putting them up at his camps at the rim above Bass Canyon and at the bottom of the Grand Canyon in Shinumo Creek. He sold his rim camp to the Santa Fe Land and Improvement Company in 1925, for $20,500. An early name for Bass Canyon was Trail Canyon. BGN 1910, 1932. (45, 54, 72)

Bass Camp is the name given the beach on the north side of the river about a mile downstream. In 1890, Robert Stanton, engineer for the Colorado River Railroad Survey, called the area Dutton's Depot Grounds for Clarence Dutton who had said, "What will you do for side track room and depot grounds along the walls of the Grand Canyon?" (94)

> *ROSS WHEELER:* This boat was built in 1914 in Green River, Utah, by Bert Loper, who named it for a murdered friend. It was abandoned in 1915 by Charles Russell, August Tadje, and Leslie Clement at the base of the Bass Trail. John Waltenberg

winched it up out of reach of flood waters where it is still visible. Kim Crumbo, NPS River Ranger, secured it with a chain in 1984. (31, 63)

MOUNT HUETHAWALI: This 6,280 ft mountain of sandstone topped with cherty limestone is the Indian name for White Mountain or Observation Point. It was also called Mount Observation. BGN 1932. (55)

HUXLEY TERRACE: Thomas Henry Huxley (1825-1895) was an English biologist and philosopher. He was called "Darwin's Bulldog" for his lectures and essays in support of Darwin's theory of evolution. It had earlier been called Observation Plateau in 1901 by George W. James. BGN 1908. (45, 55)

WALLACE BUTTE: Alfred Russell Wallace (1823-1913) was an English naturalist and explorer who simultaneously proposed with Darwin the theory of evolution by natural selection. It was earlier called Thurso Butte in 1901 after a city in Scotland by George W. James. BGN 1908. (55)

TYNDALL DOME: John Tyndall (1820-1893) was a British physicist. This feature was also called the Temple of Om in 1901 by George W. James for the largest creation of the architects of Hindustan. BGN 1908. (55)

SPENCER TERRACE: Herbert Spencer (1820-1903) was a British philosopher who developed a philosophical system with utilitarian (the idea that liberty and happiness is the goal of man) and evolutionary aspects. He was the first to use the phrase, "the survival of the fittest." It was earlier called Mystic Spring Plateau. BGN 1908. (45)

MYSTIC SPRING: This was a water source for William W. Bass for his camp on the rim. Bass was shown to the spring by his friend Captain Burro, a Havasupai. The spring was reported to have disappeared following an earthquake in the 1890s. Today, it is a wet weather seep and usually dry a majority of the year. BGN 1932. (54, 130)

FISKE BUTTE: John Fiske (1842-1901) was an American historian and writer on philosophy and science. An advocate of

Huxley and Darwin, he was also a proponent of the solar mythology theory or astrology. BGN 1908. (55)

DARWIN PLATEAU: Charles Darwin (1809-1882) was a British naturalist who proposed that species originate by descent with variation from parent forms through natural selection of those adapted to survive in the struggle for existence. BGN 1908. (45)

SIGNAL HILL: This horizontal control station was used by the USGS during topographic surveying. BGN 1932.

FOSSIL MOUNTAIN: This is a descriptive name for the abundance of fossils in the Kaibab Formation on its southwestern slope. BGN 1932.

RR   RM 107.5
HOTAUTA CANYON AND AMPHITHEATER: According to George W. James, this canyon was named for Tom Hotauta (or Hotouta), son of Navajo, the last great Havasupai chief. BGN 1910. (44, 45, 55, 56)

RL/RR   RM 108
BASS CABLE FERRY: Remains of Bass' cable, built in 1908, can be seen on both sides of the river. The cable was cut in 1968 by the NPS. (55)

RR   RM 108.5
SHINUMO CREEK, AMPHITHEATER, AND RAPIDS: Frederick Dellenbaugh, the artist on Powell's second expedition in 1871, wrote that this canyon was named by "indications of the former presence of that tribe." Powell had used the word when referring to the Hopi confederacy of Tusayan. A.H. Thompson, also on Powell's second trip and involved with surveying the area from Kanab before the expedition, called it Snake Gulch. The name was changed by 1886 on maps of the area. Shinumo is a Paiute word meaning old people or cliff dwellers. It should not be confused with Shinumo Wash located in Marble Canyon. BGN 1932. (45)

The name for Powell's Hopi confederacy of Tusayan was derived from a corruption of the Zuni word for two of the largest Hopi Towns, Usayakye, or people of Usaya, hence Tusayan. The seven cities or pueblos of Tusayan (and their translations) were: Oraibi (numerous eagle traps), Sipaulovi (place of mosquitoes), Mishongnovi (hill of boulders or the other of two sandstone columns remains standing), Shungopovi (place of chumoa, a kind of grass or reed), Sichomovi (place of the mound of the wild currant bush), Walpi (place of the gap), and Hano (the people of Hano are Tewans who moved from the Rio Grande to Tusayan during the great Pueblo revolt against Spanish authority in 1680). (45)

William W. Bass had a camp and a garden in Shinumo Creek where, after repairing prehistoric irrigation ditches, he watered his orchard of fig, peach, and apricot trees. He also grew corn, tomatoes, grapes, and melons. (45)

HOLY GRAIL TEMPLE: The Holy Grail was the cup used at the Last Supper. King Arthur's Order of the Round Table was instituted to protect the cup. When William W. Bass died in 1933, he left orders for his body to be cremated. His ashes were scattered from an airplane over the Holy Grail Temple, which had previously been known as Bass Tomb. George W. James writes, "Many years ago the first white lady to descend the canyon at this point named this 'Bass Tomb,' and I see no reason to reject the name, for in sight of it Mr. Bass' most arduous labors have been spent, and here it is appropriate he should have his immortal memorial." The lady whom James mentioned was Virginia Dox. BGN 1908. (45, 55)

DOX CASTLE: George W. James writes that this feature is named, "in honor of Miss Virginia Dox, the pioneer lady visitor to the interior of the Canyon at this point." The Dox Sandstone is named after Virginia, who was probably the first non-Indian woman to visit the Havasupai Indians in 1891. A variant name is Dox Temple. BGN 1908, 1988. (55, 121)

BURRO CANYON: This tributary to Shinumo may be named after the wild burros who used to congregate in this canyon. But more likely, it is named for Captain Burro, a Havasupai. Another Burrow Canyon is a tributary to Cove Canyon at River Mile 174.5. BGN 1910. (45, 54)

MUAV SADDLE AND CANYON: Muav is a Paiute word meaning divide or pass. Powell spoke of the canyon by name in 1869. The pass is about 5,000 ft and divides the North Rim from Powell Plateau. Muav is also the name given a Cambrian limestone layer. A variant name is Mauv Canyon, but it is not named for the color mauve, a pale bluish-purple. BGN 1910, 1988. (4, 45)

WHITE CREEK: This creek and associated trail was named by Bass after a prospector, named White, who built the upper portion of the trans-canyon Bass Trail to copper mines he had discovered in the Coconino Sandstone below Swamp Point. Bass surmised that the trail was also used by horse thieves. BGN 1932. (54, 114)

REDWALL CANYON: This a descriptive name for the Redwall Limestone which flanks the canyon. BGN 1908. (77)

FLINT CREEK: This creek received its name from the geological formations along the stream. Dark-colored chert nodules, a form of silica, are often called flint. BGN 1932. (44)

RAINBOW PLATEAU: This plateau has several points which were named by the USGS topographers for colors of the rainbow: Saffron Valley, and Violet, Emerald, and Rose Points. BGN 1908.

KING ARTHUR CASTLE: King Arthur, a British chieftain of the sixth century, and his Knights of the Round Table inspired numerous romantic tales. This and the following legendary Arthurian characters were named by Richard T. Evans, who worked with Francois E. Matthes on the topographic maps of Grand Canyon in 1902. BGN 1908. (44)

GALAHAD POINT: Sir Galahad was the purest knight of the Round Table. He was the son of Lancelot and Elaine and fated to retrieve the Holy Grail. BGN 1908. (90)

GAWAIN ABYSS: Sir Gawain was King Arthur's nephew and one of the knights of the Round Table. BGN 1908. (90)

LANCELOT POINT: Sir Lancelot was the greatest of Arthur's knights of the Round Table and the lover of Queen Guinevere. BGN 1908. (90)

GUINEVERE CASTLE: Queen Guinevere was the wife of King Arthur and Lancelot's great love. BGN 1908. (90)

ELAINE CASTLE: There are three Elaines in the Arthurian legends: the first was the "lily maid of Astolat" who pined and died for Lancelot, the second was the half sister of Arthur and mother of his son Modred, and the third was the daughter of King Pelles and the mother of Sir Galahad. BGN 1908. (90)

BEDIVERE POINT: Bedivere was the knight who brought the dying King Arthur to the barge upon which the three queens bore him to the Isle of Avalon. BGN 1908.

MERLIN ABYSS: Merlin, a semi-legendary character, figures prominently in the Round Table legends as a venerable magician and seer. BGN 1908. (90)

MODRED ABYSS: Modred (also spelled Mordred) was the treacherous nephew and killer of King Arthur. BGN 1908. (90)

EXCALIBUR: Excalibur was the magic sword that only King Arthur was able to pull from the anvil resting upon a large block of stone in a churchyard. An inscription upon the hilt prophesied that only the man who could draw out the sword should ever rule in King Uther's place. Arthur was actually the son of King Uther Pendragon, but few knew of his birth as Uther had given him to the care of the enchanter Merlin, who took him to the castle of Sir Hector, an old friend of Uther. BGN 1908. (90)

KANABOWNITS CANYON AND SPRING: Origin unknown, but kanab means willow in Paiute. BGN 1908. (45)

CRESCENT RIDGE: This is a descriptive name. BGN 1908.

MASONIC TEMPLE: George W. James named this for the Masons or Freemasons, a widely distributed secret order which promotes brotherly love among its members. The Masons arose from a class of skilled stoneworkers of the Middle Ages who possessed secret signs and passwords. BGN 1908. (45)

COPPER CANYON: This canyon was named by William W. Bass for his copper mine which he discovered with John Waltenberg about a half mile from the river. About 20-25 tons of cuprite and bornite ore were removed from the 100-125 ft deep tunnel by the partners in 1908 and transported to the rim by mule. BGN 1908. (44, 127)

EVOLUTION AMPHITHEATER: Francois Matthes named this in accordance with the noted evolutionary biologists whose names are honored nearby. See Huxley, Wallace, Spencer, Fiske, and Darwin. BGN 1908.

HAKATAI CANYON AND RAPIDS: Bass and Waltenberg discovered asbestos in this canyon in the Bass Limestone. Several tons of 1-4 inch fibers were packed out of the canyon and sold in 1917. It was shipped to Europe and used to fire-proof theater curtains. Hakatai is from the Havasupai name for Grand Canyon, Hackataia, meaning any large, roaring sound, whether caused by a fierce wind or the dashing of the waters. BGN 1932. (45, 54)

FAN ISLAND: This is a descriptive name for the shape of the flat-topped fan-shaped butte. (45)

KING CREST: Clarence King (1842-1901) was an American geologist who lead the War Department's Survey along the Fortieth Parallel. He described the mineral resources along the route of the Union Pacific Railroad and exposed the Great Diamond Hoax. He was the first Director of the USGS from 1878 to 1881, and was among the first to use contour lines in map making. BGN 1908. (5)

WALTHENBERG CANYON AND RAPIDS: This canyon is named for John Waltenberg (spelled Walthenberg by the BGN), who was originally from Wisconsin. He was a mining employee and/or partner of William W. Bass for 18 years. Bass's second son in his remembrances of early childhood in Grand Canyon said, "John Waltenberg was a mystery. I don't know where he came from or how he tied up with my Dad, whether they were partners or what. He just depended on my Dad to look after him. I always felt bad about John; he never realized anything from all those years of work, except a case of 'Star' chewing tobacco now and then." Waltenberg also worked for Levi F. Noble on the Shinumo Quadrangle area survey and it was Noble who recommended the spelling of his name as Walthenberg. Variant spellings include Waltenburg and Walthenburg. The Kolb brothers called the rapid "Christmas Rapid" when they ran the rapid on December 24, 1911. While running the rapid, the *Defiance,* Ellsworth's boat, tipped over and Emery's boat, the *Edith*, had a hole bashed in the side. The *Edith*, named after Emery's daughter, was repaired on Christmas day. BGN 1964. (45, 54, 60, 72)

> **DUTTON POINT AND CANYON:** George W. James named these features for Major Clarence Edward Dutton (1841-1912), a career soldier with the United States Army, who accompanied the Powell Survey in 1875. He wrote for the Government a monograph called the *Tertiary History of the Grand Canyon District*. He joined geology to chemistry, geophysics, and landscape esthetics. Dutton had an interest in oriental religions and began the tradition of naming features in the canyon for mythologic deities. He saw resemblances between the great buttes in the canyon with temples in India and China and often used architectural terms in naming them. BGN 1932. (36, 45)

RC   RM 113
113 MILE ROCK: The rock in mid-channel has no name. An early 1970s ARTA (American River Touring Association) river trip called it Rancid Tuna Fish Sandwich Rock, but the name is not commonly used by river runners.

RL   RM 114.5
GARNET CANYON: William W. Bass named this canyon. Garnet is a mineral with a deep-red color used as a gem or an abrasive. BGN 1908. (44)

> **DRUMMOND PLATEAU:** Henry Drummond (1851-1897) was a Scottish clergyman and writer. BGN 1908.

> **CHEMEHUEVI POINT:** Chemehuevi is a Yuman word for Paiute Indian. The Chemehuevi Indians lived along the Colorado River and aided Lt. Amiel W. Whipple's expedition. BGN 1908. (90)

MONUMENT FOLD: This small monoclinal bend or fold and associated minor faulting in the Tapeats Sandstone is located below Explorers Monument, thus the name.

> **EXPLORERS MONUMENT:** This honors the explorers of the Grand Canyon: Lt. Joseph C. Ives, Lt. George M. Wheeler, Lt. Edward F. Beale, Dr. Almon H. Thompson, and Dr. John Newberry. Who named Explorers Monument is unknown. George Wharton James suggested that the explorers were the Spanish conquistadors and padres whose names are honored on the terraces downstream. It was earlier called Marcos Monument by George W. James for Fray Marcos de Niza. BGN 1908. (55)

ROYAL ARCH CREEK: The creek is named for Royal Arch, a 60 foot span located a quarter mile up from the mouth, which can not be seen from the river. BGN 1908. (19)

> **ELVES CHASM:** This perennial, spring-fed, travertine chasm is filled with ferns, cardinal monkey flowers, columbines, and orchids. A visit to it is like a visit to fairyland where the elves live. BGN 1908. (45)

> **AZTEC AMPHITHEATER:** The Aztec empire, dominant in Central Mexico, was present at the time of the Spanish invasion in 1519. This and the following Aztec names were applied by the government surveyors. BGN 1908. (90)

> **TOLTEC POINT:** The Toltec Indians of Mexico, who lived prior to the Aztec Indians, may have lived as far north as the Gila River in Arizona. A variant spelling is Toteo Point. BGN 1908. (45, 146)

> **MONTEZUMA POINT:** Montezuma II (1477-1520) was the Aztec emperor of Mexico who was conquered by Cortez and killed in a revolt by his own subjects. BGN 1908. (90)

> **POINT HUITZIL:** Huitzil is the name of a Mexican tribe. BGN 1908. (44)

CENTEOTL POINT: Centeotl, sometimes spelled Centeoti or Ceyotl, is a word in the Nahuatl language (a Uto-Aztecan language group). Ceyotl is derived from Coytl, from which we derive the word coyote. BGN 1908, 1961. (44)

POINT QUETZAL: The quetzal is a Central American bird which has golden-green and scarlet plumage. The male has long tail feathers and is the national bird of Guatemala. Quetzalcoatl was the principal deity of the Aztecs. BGN 1908. (90)

APACHE POINT AND TERRACE: The Spanish explorer Espejo first called the Indians, Apichi in 1581. By 1799, Apache was applied to the following Indian groups: Tonto, Chiricahua, Gileno, Mimbreno, Taracone, Mescalero, Lipane, Llanero, and Navajo. The term means strangers or enemy. At this point, George W. James reported that the Havasupais would throw off captured Apache warriors. BGN 1932. (45, 55)

RM 117 to 119

STEPHEN AISLE: Stephen is an anglicization of Esteban or Estevan, but who named it is unknown. Esteban was the black, Christianized Moor from Morocco, who with Andres Dorantes, Cabeza de Vaca, and Alfonso de Castillo were the only survivors of 400 men from Panfilo de Narvaez's Florida expedition of 1528. After much travail, they found their way overland to Mexico City and told of the fabulous wealth of cities they had passed. This report was similar to that of Nuno Beltran de Guzman who heard from an Indian in 1529 that seven rich cities were in northern "New Spain." This matched the medieval tale of Seven Cities of Antilia, founded by seven Christian bishops who fled across the sea to escape the conquering Moslems. In 1539, Esteban, acting as the guide, journeyed ahead of Fray Marcos de Niza's expedition to search for the gold. He sent back an Indian with a message that the seven cities had buildings which were two to three stories high and rich in turquoise. The Zuni Indians later told the Spaniards that the arrogant Esteban had been slain in Hawikuh. An aisle is a wing or lateral division of a church on either side of the nave. Stephen Aisle was earlier called the Aisle of Cardenas by George W. James. BGN 1908. (55, 103)

MARCOS TERRACE: This terrace is named by the USGS cartographers who mapped the canyon in 1927. Fray Marcos de Niza was dispatched by Antonio de Mendoza in 1539, the viceroy of New Spain, as Mexico was then called, as an envoy to find the great cities of Cibola and plunder the treasure. Cibola is an anglicization of the Zuni name for themselves (Shivona) and also the name of their last pueblo. After hearing of Esteban's death, Marcos viewed the cities from afar, then returned and reported that he has seen seven golden cities in the distance. A variant name is Coronado Plateau. BGN 1908. (45, 103)

DE VACA TERRACE: Alvar Nunez Cabeza de Vaca was one of the surviving remnant of the Panfilo de Narvaez's Spanish Expeditionary force which explored the coastline from Tampa Bay to Galveston in 1528, 32 years after Columbus discovered America. They were lost for two years and from 1534-1536 made the long walk from Galveston across Texas and New Mexico to the west coast of Mexico. They finally reunited with the Spanish Forces in New Spain, as Mexico was then called. De Vaca reported to Viceroy Antonio de Mendoza of the existence of great cities in the headwaters of the Rio Grande which contained fabulous wealth. The terrace was named in 1906 by Francois Matthes. BGN 1908. (45, 103)

WHEELER POINT: Lt. George Montague Wheeler was in charge of the War Department's Geographical Surveys West of the One Hundredth Meridian. On October 19, 1871, he reached Diamond Creek after 33 days using Mohave Indian laborers to drag three boats 200 miles upstream from Camp Mohave. The boats returned in five days. BGN 1908. (5, 45, 54)

RR   RM 120

BLACKTAIL CANYON AND VALLEY: Blacktail was named by Frank Bond in 1932 for the valley above. Blacktail refers to the mule deer, a species who are especially numerous on the Kaibab Plateau and used to be called Rocky Mountail blacktail in the early 1900s. Mule deer are large deer with large ears. Their tail is white or tan but conspicuously tipped with black. During winter, mule deer must move down from the snowy high country to canyons where there is ample yard, or winter pasture and browsing ground. Blacktail deer, a separate species, are found in the Pacific northwest. BGN 1908, 1932. (2, 52)

RM 120 to 123

CONQUISTADOR AISLE: The aisle honors the conquistadors, the 16th Century Spanish explorers and conquerors of North and South

America. The term comes from the Spanish verb conquistar, meaning to conquer. On the original Shinumo Quadrangle map, this aisle is called Alarcon Aisle, a name given by George. W. James in 1901. Francois Matthes in 1906 suggested that Cardenas Aisle (now known of Stephens Aisle) together with Alarcon Aisle be united in a single, collective name, Explorers Canyon, but the name Conquistador was finally chosen. BGN 1906. (45, 55)

TOBAR TERRACE: Pedro de Tobar (also spelled Tovar, as in the El Tovar Hotel, built on the South Rim in 1905), was a Lieutenant under Francisco Vasquez de Coronado. He was dispatched to investigate Tusayan, or Old Oraibi. Coronado thought that Tusayan could be similar to the Zuni's Seven Cities of Cibola, but Tobar found them to be just more adobe pueblo villages. The Hopis told Tobar of another Indian tribe (presumably the Havasupai) who lived near a great river to the west. BGN 1908. (45)

ALARCON TERRACE: In May 1540, Captain Hernando Alarcon was assigned by Antonio de Mendoza, Cortez's successor, to take supplies to the Coronado Expedition via the Gulf of California and up the Colorado River. He arrived at the head of the Gulf on August 26, 1540, and convinced the Cocopah Indians that he was the son of the sun god. The Cocopahs helped him tow his boats up the river to the vicinity of the present day Yuma, where he failed to meet Coronado. He named the Colorado River, El Rio de Buena Guia (The River of Good Guidance). BGN 1908. (45, 54)

IVES POINT: In 1857, Lt. Joseph Christmas Ives on the steamboat *Explorer* traveled upstream from the Colorado River delta 350 miles to Black Canyon. He traveled overland to Diamond Creek and commented, "The region is, of course, altogether valueless. It can be approached only from the south, and after entering it there is nothing to do but leave. Ours has been the first, and will doubtless be the last, party of whites to visit this profitless locality. It seems intended by nature that the Colorado River, along the greater portion of its lonely and majestic way, shall be forever unvisited and undisturbed." BGN 1908. (45, 54)

FORSTER CANYON AND RAPIDS: W.J. Forster, who died in 1925, worked on the USGS topographic survey of the Supai Quadrangle along this part of the Colorado River. He walked here from Elves Chasm in 1904. This is also the site where Ed Hudson's *Esmeralda II* was found on river left by Jim Rigg and Frank Wright. See Willie's Necktie Rapids. BGN 1925. (44, 130)

> **ENFILADE POINT:** This point is located in a sharp bend of the river and can be seen at the end of Conquistador Aisle on the South Rim. An Indian ruin is located on a detached promontory at Enfilade Point. Blocks of limestone form a parapet on the side that faces the mainland. Enfilade is gunfire directed from the side at a line of troops or a position held by soldiers where they would be exposed to such raking gunfire. BGN 1932.

FOSSIL CANYON, BAY, AND RAPIDS: The Havasupais used to farm the delta at Fossil Canyon. The name was submitted by the USGS on a 1927 map for the many fossil remains and shells found in the rock of the canyon. BGN 1932. (44)

> **STANTON POINT:** Robert Brewster Stanton (d. 1922) was chief engineer of the 1889 river-level survey route for F.M. Brown's Denver, Colorado Canyon, and Pacific Railroad Company. Stanton had designed the famous Georgetown Loop in Colorado and believed the project could be done. After the deaths of Brown, Hansbrough, and Richards in upper Marble Canyon, he returned three months later and completed the trip to the Gulf of California in 1890. His was the second expedition after Powell to complete the journey down the Green and Colorado Rivers. Afterwards, the investors of the railway project declined to support the project. BGN 1925. (45, 94)

> **GREAT THUMB MESA AND POINT:** This descriptive name was suggested by Frank Bond as it looks like a huge thumb from the air. BGN 1932. (4, 45)

GARCES TERRACE: In 1776, Fray Francisco Tomas Garces made an exploratory and missionary expedition and visited the Hualapai, the Havasupai, and Hopi Indians. BGN 1908. (45, 54)

BEALE POINT: Lt. Edward Fitzgerald "Ned" Beale (1822-1893) surveyed a wagon route from Fort Defiance to the Colorado River across northern Arizona in 1857. He used 25 camels to carry supplies. BGN 1908. (45)

THOMPSON POINT: Dr. Almon H. Thompson was married to Powell's sister, Ellen Louella, known as Nell or Nellie. Originally an entomologist and school superintendent, Powell chose him to be the astronomer, head geographer, and second-in-command on the second Powell expedition in 1871-1872. He was called "the Professor" by the crew. He became the Chief Geographer of the USGS from 1879-1906. BGN 1908.

NEWBERRY POINT: Dr. John Strong Newberry (1822-1892) was a surgeon and geologist on the Ives expedition in 1857-1858. BGN 1906. (54)

RL   RM 126.5

RANDYS ROCK: An ARTA raft (22 ft snout rig) wrecked on this rock in June 1976. Randy Breckenridge, the boatman, and six others were napping after a morning spent at Elves Chasm, while Freddie Bendheim, a passenger was rowing. The raft wrapped on the Tapeats block on river left, dumping everyone in the river save for one fellow who climbed up on the rock. Trip leader Peter Winn, then 26 years old, swam to the rock and with the marooned passenger spent an hour trying to cut off as much gear as possible. The 12-day trip to Diamond Creek continued with 11 passengers on each of the two remaining rafts. The meat cooler was salvaged and flotsam was found in eddies below or delivered by passing motor boats. When Rob Elliott, the owner, picked up the trip at Diamond Creek he was convinced that the missing boat was a practical joke, until the loaded trailer drove away from the river, minus the raft. (136)

                                                          RM 127 to 131

MIDDLE GRANITE GORGE: Middle Granite Gorge is four miles long and reaches from about 127 Mile Creek to below Bedrock Canyon. BGN 1925.

RL   RM 129

SPECTER CHASM, TERRACE, AND RAPIDS: The name was proposed by the USGS in 1908, presumably for the dark, sinister, and spooky schist which helps to create a forbidding atmosphere. Clyde

Eddy, on his 1927 trip, wrote that at Specter Chasm, "The canyon that the river has cut through the granite becomes an inner gorge - a narrow, dismal trench where a thousand dangers threaten and from which escape is impossible in case of shipwreck." BGN 1908, 1932. (37)

RR   RM 130

130 MILE CREEK: A spectacular waterfall spilling over from the rocks above is sometimes called the Four Second Waterfall by river guides as it is visible only briefly from the river.

RR   RM 130.5

BEDROCK CANYON AND RAPIDS: This canyon was named by Frank Bond for the exposed bedrock island of Precambrian granite in the rapid below. BGN 1932. (45)

> **DOLLS HOUSE:** River runners call this diminutive jungle-gym in the schist the Doll's House as it reminds guides of the colorful crags, twisting tunnels, and pointed pinnacles of the Doll House, which is located in Canyonlands National Park above Spanish Bottom, below the confluence of the Green and the Colorado Rivers in Utah. (97)

RR   RM 131.5

GALLOWAY CANYON: This is named to honor Nathaniel Galloway (also called Than, 1860-1913) who pioneered the stern first style of rowing and was the first person to run the Grand Canyon twice. Oarsmen of Powell and Stanton trips, in typical row boat fashion, sat facing upstream at the stern of the boat with their backs and the bow of the boat to the direction of travel. Galloway ran stern first, facing downstream.[2] He also built Cataract style boats, which were commonly 16 ft long, narrow of beam, and shallow with square sterns and a pronounced rake. Galloway and William Richmond, a beaver trapper from Utah, successfully navigated the Colorado River from near Green River, Wyoming to Needles, California from September 1896 to

---

[2]George Flavel pioneered the style used by river runners today. He rowed bow first, facing downstream. Flavell and Ramon Montez journeyed down the Colorado River a few months before Galloway's 1896 first trip. Flavell was remarkable in that he claims in his account of the trip (*The Log of the Panthon*) to have run all the rapids but Soap Creek, thus making him the first to run Hance Rapids and Lava Falls. His trip through the Grand Canyon lasted 14 days (Oct. 17-30) from Lee's Ferry to the Grand Wash Cliffs. The journey ended at Yuma. No life preservers were taken on the trip. (41,63)

February 1897. He later worked for Stanton dredging gold in Glen Canyon and met the drilling company's president, Julius Stone. He joined Stone, Dubendorff, Cogswell and Sharp for Stone's 1909 expedition. A variant misspelled name is Gazzoway. BGN 1932. (45, 63, 127)

ARROWHEAD TERRACE: Frank Bond named this spur as it looks like an Indian arrowhead from the air. (4, 45)

RM 131.5

DEUBENDORFF RAPIDS: Seymour Sylvester "Dubie" Dubendorff (spelled Deubendorff by BGN) was working as a handy-man on the Vernal, Utah, weekly newspaper when he met and joined Julius Stone's 1909 expedition from Green River, Wyoming, to Needles, California. Dubie was not a boatman, but amiable, skilled in other outdoor pursuits, strong as an ox, and in Stone's words, "gritty as a flapjack rolled in sand." The 27 year old Dubie was the first to flip in this rapid and the USGS 1923 survey named the rapid and the side canyons above and below to commemorate the incident. Dubendorf wrote in his journal, "...I followed into the high waves and rougher water. In the very trough of one of these waves a rock lay in my path which I struck squarely with the stern of my boat. This capsized me and when I rose I struck the gunwale of my boat with my head, cutting quite a gash. I swam to one side and rising again came up free from the boat. I then swam for shore and was carried down stream 250 to 300 yards, most of this time under the water. I would catch my breath in the trough of each wave. Everything came out all right, even my cap was picked up. The boat was jammed in the stern and fore curtain torn. One of my extra oars was broken off above the blade. I bruised or sprained my knee in the river." Dubie died the following year of Rocky Mountain spotted fever. (35, 63, 98)

RR   RM 132

STONE CREEK: Julius Stone was an Ohio manufacturer, who became president of Stanton's Glen Canyon gold mining venture. He hired Galloway to design and supervise building of four boats and floated from Green River, Wyoming, to Needles, California in ten weeks. His 1909 expedition is called the first sportsman's river trip. In 1932, he published a book about the trip called, *Canyon Country: The Romance of a Drop of Water and a Grain of Sand*. BGN 1932. (63, 98)

STEAMBOAT MOUNTAIN: This is a descriptive name for the 7,410 ft peak which can be seen from the river upstream of Specter and Bedrock Rapids, for it looks to some like a steamboat. (4, 56)

RR   RM 133.5

TAPEATS CREEK, TERRACE, AMPHITHEATER, CAVE, AND TERRACE: Tapeats was named by Powell for Ta Pits, a Paiute who claimed ownership of the drainage when he pointed it out to Powell from the Kaibab Plateau. Over 6,000 ft of passageways have been explored in Tapeats Cave. Typical flow of Tapeats Creek when not in flood is about 79 cfs. BGN 1932. (19, 33, 45, 134)

> **THUNDER RIVER AND SPRING:** The sound of the water as it explodes from the Redwall and Muav Limestones, gives the river its name. The half-mile Thunder River is a minor tributary to Tapeats Creek, as well as one of the shortest rivers in the world. Over 3,000 ft of passageways have been charted behind the waterfall.
>
> The water comes from rain and snow which fall on the Kaibab Plateau. Falling rain dissolves carbon dioxide from the atmosphere, creating carbonic acid. This acid rain chemically weathers limestone or carbonate rocks when it pools on the rock and passes underground through sinks and joints into caverns. Sinks are created when the underground caverns honeycomb an area creating weak spots which then collapse. The groundwater drops to the water table or flows out in giant springs if an impermeable layer is reached. Sinks and caverns under limestone surfaces are collectively called karst topography by geologists. BGN 1932. (4, 19)
>
> **SURPRISE VALLEY:**   E.O. Beaman, photographer and boatman on the *Canonita* on Powell's second expedition, walked upstream from Kanab Creek to Deer Creek with George Riley during mid-April, 1872. After climing upstream a short distance until their path was blocked by the canyon wall, they scaled a cliff to the first main ledge and beheld a verdant basin which they named Surprise Valley. This area was probablly the upper valley of Deer Creek. The hanging valley above Deer Creek came to be known as Surprise Valley, with its unusual bowl

shape and nearly hidden outlet through Bonita Creek. (36, 92b, 96)

BRIDGERS KNOLL: Jim Bridger (1804-1881) was a mountain man, fur trader, frontiersman, and scout. He established a trading post on the Black Fork of the Green River from 1843-1853. Mormons squeezed him out after they accused him of selling guns to the Indians. He also set up a waystation, called Fort Bridger, for emigrants on the Oregon Trail and guided the Berthoud party from Denver to the Great Salt Lake. He married three successive Indian wives.

MONUMENT POINT: This point, visible from the river, was named by Powell in 1883. The Bill Hall Trail drops down to the Esplanade from Monument Point. Hall, a 24 year old seasonal Park Ranger at Grand Canyon, was killed in a highway accident on North Rim in 1979. (124)

CRAZY JUG CANYON AND POINT: This is named for a curiously shaped rock, called the Crazy Jug. (81)

PARISSAWAMPITTS SPRING AND POINT: Dutton named this in 1882 after the Paiute word parush meaning flowing or boiling water, in reference to the spring which bubbles or boils out of the ground. The meaning of the last part of the name is unknown. (36)

FENCE POINT: This is a descriptive name for the fence between the Kaibab National Forest and Grand Canyon National Park.

TIMP CANYON AND POINT: Origin unknown. BGN 1932.

STINA CANYON AND POINT: Origin unknown. BGN 1932.

SADDLE CANYON: This refers to Muav Saddle which separates the Tapeats and Shinumo watersheds. The other Saddle Canyon is upstream in Marble Canyon. BGN 1932.

CASTLE CANYON: This is a descriptive name. BGN 1932.

FIRE POINT: Fire Point was named by the NPS in 1932. The Park started keeping fire records in 1926. Since that time, fires on North Rim have increased during the summer months when lightening strikes ignite the dry forest and underlying needles and duff. Stephen Pyne's *Fire on the Rim: A Firefighter's Season at the Grand Canyon* is an excellent book on the subject. BGN 1932. (44, 84)

SWAMP POINT: In 1908, the USGS named this Tulip Point, but it was renamed Swamp Point in 1932, upon recommendation of then Superintendent Tillotson due to common usage and its proximity to Swamp Lake, an intermittent lake on the Kaibab Plateau. Local cowboys called it Fen Lake. Fen is another word for a marsh, swamp, or bog. (44)

RR   RM 134.5
BONITA CREEK: Origin unknown. Bonita is Spanish for pretty.

RL   RM 134.5
OWL CAMP AND CANYON: This common name was given by river runners to the riverside camp and unnamed canyon for the two large alcoves in the Kaibab Limestone at the rim which look like owl eyes.

RL   RM 135
HELICOPTER EDDY: This eddy on river left earns its name as it is an almost constant whirlpool at most river levels.

                                                                RM 135 to 136
GRANITE NARROWS: C.H. Birdseye, of the 1923 USGS Expedition, wrote in his journal of September 10, "...the granite dips up for about 3/4 mile only. At the entrance to this short granite gorge the walls are only about 75 feet apart. We name this point Granite Narrows." It is sometimes called the Little Granite Narrows. BGN 1932. (10)

COGSWELL BUTTE: Raymond Austin Cogswell (1873-1964) was an expert photographer and Julius Stone's brother-in-law. While on Stone's 1909 expedition, he took over 2,000 pictures. BGN 1966. (98)

CHRISTMAS TREE CAVE: This large cavern at the contact of the granite and the overlying Grand Canyon Series has a stalagmite of calcium carbonate which looks like a miniature

Christmas tree. It was named by a Grand Canyon Expeditions boatman in 1971. The floor of the cave is covered with bat guano. (97)

RR   RM 136
DEER CREEK AND FALLS: A prospector had told E.O. Beaman about a waterfall beside the Colorado River. So in mid-April 1872, Beaman and George Riley hiked upstream from Kanab Creek to Deer Creek to photograph the scene. Beaman named the waterfall, Buckskin Cascade, though it is now called Deer Creek Falls. They called the waterfall Buckskin Falls. Beaman constructed a small log raft and floated alone back to Kanab Creek. He returned a few days later with Samuel Rudd, a miner, to take pictures. Robert Stanton called the waterfall Bridle or Bridal Falls, while the Kolb brothers called it Surprise Falls. BGN 1964. Deer Creek was probably named for the presence of mule deer. (60, 92b, 94, 96)

>   **DEER SPRING:** This is a descriptive name for the mule deer which can sometimes be seen in the valley. River runners sometimes call this spring, Dutton Spring, after Clarence Dutton, the geologist. In 1880, Dutton traveled down by horse to Deer Creek on a trail built by prospectors in 1876.

>   **VAUGHN SPRING:** Origin unknown.

RL   RM 136.5
PONCHOS KITCHEN: This overhang campsite is called Poncho's Kitchen or Patio by river guides. Ringtailed cats, members of the Raccoon Family, are especially common here. They are nocturnal and omnivorous. (52)

                                                               RM 137.5
DORIS RAPIDS: Doris Drown Nevills (1914-1949), wife of Norm Nevills, was swept overboard by a wave in this rapid, then rescued on a 1940 river trip. Norm credited Doris as being good natured and uncomplaining, able to read water better than he, and a menu and food planning expert. (23, 31)

RR   RM 139
FISHTAIL CANYON, POINT, AND FAULT: This is a descriptive name for the two points at the north rim east of Kanab Creek. BGN 1932. (45)

105

140 MILE CANYON: C.H. Birdseye, of the 1923 USGS Expedition, called this canyon "Neighing Horse Canyon." BGN 1932. (10)

> **KEYHOLE NATURAL BRIDGE:** A bridge up a side tributary was discovered and named by P.T. Reilly from an aerial photo he had taken of the area in 1956 while flying with Martin Litton, river runner, environmentalist, and original owner of the commercial company called Grand Canyon Dories. (117)

> **TAHUTA TERRACE AND POINT:** Tahuta is Havasupai for hidden or something concealed. The point was named in 1925 for Eunice Tahuta Jones (1876-1964), a respected Havasupai woman and basketmaker. BGN 1925, 1932. (74)

> **GATAGAMA TERRACE AND POINT:** Gatagama is a Havasupai family name. The family helped to develop the tourist trade in the 1880s. BGN 1925. (44, 45)

KANAB CREEK, CANYON, PLATEAU, AND POINT: Kanab is a Paiute word for the willow which grow throughout the canyon. Powell's second trip abandoned the expedition via this canyon on September 8, 1872 when Powell announced, "Well, boys, our voyage is done!" Dellenbaugh states that the high water and the possibility of attack by the Paiute Indians influenced Powell's decision. After Powell made his announcement, Jack Hillers, the photographer on the trip wrote that, "Everybody felt like praising God." A fine flour gold was found here in 1871 by George Riley, a prospector who accompanied Powell's overland survey reconnaissance and was his cook for the New Year's dinner at Lee's Ferry. News of the discovery launched a four month goldrush the next year. BGN 1932, 1974. (32, 33, 45, 54)

> **WHISPERING FALLS:** Origin unknown, it is a descriptive name used by river runners.

> **RACETRACK KNOLL:** This descriptive name is used as the area around the knoll looks like a racetrack. It is located at the Hermit Shale and Esplanade Sandstone contact where the Esplanade Sandstone forms the racetrack surface. (130)

JUMPUP CANYON: The name may be derived from the sharp drop in the bed of the drainage which hikers or horses have to jump up. This canyon was called Stewart's Ranch and Stewart Canyon by Powell's second expedition. (1, 131)

KWAGUNT HOLLOW: This is named after Kwagunt, a Paiute Indian. See Kwagunt Canyon. BGN 1964. (43, 58)

INDIAN HOLLOW: A band of Kaibab Paiute Indians lived nearby. (58)

SOWATS CANYON: This is an anglicized Paiute word for a plant which that tribe smoked, as tobacco is used today. The variant name is Showap. (110)

CHAMBERLAIN CANYON: This canyon may be named for Thomas Chamberlain, bishop and president of the United Order of Orderville in 1876, a Mormon cooperative. (1)

HACKS CANYON: This honors the early settler of the region, Haskell "Hack" Jolly. He bought the spring in the canyon from Chris Heaton and raised horses here for many years. (110)

PAGUEKWASH POINT: Paguekwash is from the Paiute word paguek, a family name meaning fish tail. It is descriptive for the shape of the mesa as seen from above or the shape of the canyon below as it branches like a fish's tail. BGN 1925. (45)

RL   RM 145.5

OLO CANYON: Olo is a shortened form of the Havasupai word vo-olo-o meaning horse. Their word comes from caballo, the Spanish word for horse. In 1776, Garces recorded that the Havasupai had horses and cattle, apparently received in trade from the Hopis. Olo-oqlace means little horses. In 1938, rumors of little horses in Havasu reached the NPS, but they turned out to be 300 pound Indian ponies stunted from poor desert grazing. BGN 1925. (54, 107)

HAMIDREEK POINT: Hamidreek is a Havasupai family name meaning nighthawk. It is sometimes spelled Hamtecq or Hamidrik. BGN 1988. (74)

KANGAROO HEADLAND: This headland resembles a kangaroo in outline. Frank Bond suggested the name in 1929. BGN 1932. (4, 45)

CHIKAPANAGI MESA AND POINT: This mesa, between Olo and Matakatamiba Canyons, was named by George W. James. It is the Havasupai Indian word for bat, meaning they who moved a man down. Chikapanagi was an Indian friend of William W. Bass who received his name from the striking similarity his face at times had to that of a bat. BGN 1925, 1932, 1988. (55, 107)

MATKATAMIBA CANYON: This is a Havasupai family name. Mat means earth or dirt. Variant names are Matkatameeba and Natkatameeba. BGN 1925, 1932. (45, 107)

PANAMETA POINT AND TERRACE: This is a Havasupai family name. BGN 1925, 1932. (45)

MOUNT AKABA: A Havasupai family by this name lived near this butte. BGN 1925. (45)

PAYA POINT: This is named for Lemuel J. Paya, a Havasupai. Paya was once a member of the Supai Tribal Council and a spokesman for the tribe. BGN 1925. (45)

PANYA POINT: This is a Havasupai family name. BGN 1925. (45)

TOWAGO POINT: This is a Havasupai family name. BGN 1925. (45)

UPSET RAPIDS AND 150 MILE CANYON: This was named by Colonel Birdseye during the 1923 USGS trip when Emery Kolb flipped or upset his boat, the *Marble*. Jesse "Shorty" Burton also capsized his motor boat in Upset Rapids on June 14, 1967. His life jacket became caught and he drowned. No one else in the party was hurt. At that time, the pontoon boat called a tail dragger, was run without the side tubes and the motor was mounted outside the tube. The guide's legs were wedged under crossed ropes and the rear section of the tube was somewhat deflated so as to keep the prop in the water if a short shaft motor was used. The canyon has also been called S B Canyon, a name given to the west fork. BGN 1925, 1964. (63, 148)

> **BOYSAG POINT AND RIM:** Boysag is a Paiute word for bridge. This point, on the North Rim of Grand Canyon can only be reached by crossing a small, artificial bridge. BGN 1925 (45)

> **SHANUB POINT:** This may be the Paiute word for dog. BGN 1925. (45)

> **DEAD HORSE MESA:** Origin unknown, but probably in reference to a dead horse being found here.

RL   RM 150.5
UPSET HOTEL: This is the name given by river runners for the camp below Upset Rapids. Many a trip, after flipping in Upset Rapids, has recovered here on the strip of sand hidden behind the rocky shoreline.

RR   RM 151.5
LEDGES: This is the name given by river runners to the Muav Limestone ledge camp. It had earlier been slightly upstream, but a rock fall relocated the camp.

RL   RM 153.5
SINYELLA CANYON, MESA, MOUNT, AND RAPIDS: Havasupai chief Judge Sinyella (1853-1923) owned the upper part of Havasu Canyon to Bass' Camp on the South Rim. He sold a horse, Silver, and a red mule to Bass. Sinyella was the principal informant to Leslie Spier of the American Museum of Natural History who studied the life and traditions of the Havasupai from 1918-1920. The spelling was changed in 1988 to Sinyella (from Sinyala or Sinyela) to reflect proper Havasupai spelling. Sinyella means to part by a forward movement. Mount Sinyella is visible from the river near River Mile 152. The name was suggested by Charles Sheldon. BGN 1988. (45, 56, 95, 127)

RR   RM 155
This canyon has no official name, but is called various names by river runners, among them Paradise, Pete's Pocket, and Slime Canyon. A lovely waterfall spills over the lip of the canyon into the river below. A bronze memorial plaque to a German hiker is placed here.

LAST CHANCE: This camp on the Muav Limestone ledges was named by river runners as it is the "last chance" to camp before Havasu Canyon. Campsites are few and far between from Deer Creek to Havasu Creek. This section of river is sometimes called the Ice Box as it is nearly always in the shade.

HAVASU CANYON, CREEK, FALLS, AND SPRING: Fray Francisco Tomas Garces reached Havasu Canyon on June 20, 1776 and called the creek Rio Jebesua and Rio de San Antonio. Ives called it Cataract and Cascade River. Today, the portion of the drainage from 5 miles northwest of the city of Williams to Havasu Springs below Hualapai Canyon is called Cataract Canyon. Below that, the next 10 miles to the Colorado River is called Havasu Canyon. (45)

Havasu receives its name from a Havasupai word which has two meanings. Most commonly it is translated as people of the blue-green waters. But, it is also interpreted as the people who live at the place which is green, in reference to the green vegetation which is supported by the perennial stream. Havasu means the color blue or green, but not blue-green. Ha is part of a color term, while pai means people. River guides often call the canyon Havazoo, for the menagerie of people and crowded mooring in the mouth of the canyon during the summer months. Variant names include Cactus Canyon and Cataract Creek. BGN 1932, 1964. (54, 107)

Silver, carbonate of lead, and vanadium were found here in 1873 by Charles Spencer. In 1879, a lead-silver claim was made at the base of Havasu Falls (then called Bridal Veil Falls). The song "From the Land of Sky Blue Water" by Charles Cadman is said to have been written about Havasu Creek, but it is actually based on an Omaha tribal melody and poem by Nelle Ebehart. (28, 54)

Floods in Havasu Canyon are episodic. A 20 ft wall of flood water swept through the village on January 3, 1910. A recent flood on September 3, 1990, studied by the USGS, placed a discharge of 22,800 cfs based upon high water marks. A 12 to 14 ft wall of water swept through Supai Village, Mooney Falls was lowered by many feet, travertine terraces were removed, and Velvet Ash trees a foot or more in diameter were swept downstream from Havasu Creek to Lake Mead. The trail was rebuilt in the spring of 1991. The flood frequency recurrence interval of Havasu Canyon is between 25 and 50 years. The typical flow of Havasu Creek is about 50 cfs. (45, 86, 134)

BEAVER CANYON AND FALLS: George W. James writes that, "About six miles below Mooney Falls is a smaller cataract named Beaver Falls, from the large number of beaver constantly at work there." BGN 1932. (45, 55)

YUNOSI CANYON AND POINT: This is a Havasupai family name. There are two origin stories centered on a play on the phrase, "You no see." One story is that mapmakers did not discover the area adjacent to Beaver and Little Coyote Canyons until the mid-1920s. The other is that the grieving wife of Chief Hotouta received that name after she had visions of his ghost or spirit and in her broken English cried to on-lookers, "You no see? You no see?" (45)

MOONEY FALLS: Richard Evans named this for James (also listed as Daniel W.) Mooney who lost his life here in 1880. Once a sailor who grew weary of that life, he settled in Prescott and became a miner. He dropped to his death while scaling down the falls on a rope that was too short. His body was recovered ten months later (supposedly preserved by the travertine spray) and buried. George W. James said the Havasupais called the falls Mother of the Waters. The falls were also called Hualapai Falls. BGN 1925. (45, 55)

The other waterfalls are called Havasu (also known as Bridal Veil), Navajo (BGN 1932), and Fiftyfoot Falls (also known as Supai Falls, BGN 1932). (45, 127)

UQUALLA POINT: This is a Havasupai family name, sometimes spelled Ukwalla. BGN 1988. (45)

CARBONATE CANYON: Calcium carbonate is dissolved from limestone layers, transported by spring and ground water, and redeposited as travertine. BGN 1932.

MULGULLO POINT: This is a Havasupai family name. BGN 1925.

MANAKACHA POINT: This is a Havasupai family name, sometimes spelled Manakaja, meaning who cares for his children. When Chief Jasper Manakaja (1850-1942) died, he was survived by two sons, one daughter, 21 grandchildren, 25 great grandchildren, and five great great grandchildren. BGN 1925. (74)

TITHUMIGI POINT: This is a Havasupai family name. BGN 1925. (45)

MOUNT WODO: This butte was named in 1925 by the USGS for a Havasupai family. BGN 1925. (45)

PUTESOY CANYON: This is a Havasupai family name which many mean coyote, though the word kathad is typically their term for the animal. BGN 1988. (45, 107)

SUPAI VILLAGE: The name for the village of Supai is shortened from Havasupai, meaning people who live where it is green or people of the blue-green water. (45, 107)

WIGLEEYA: Wigleeya (or Wigeleeva) are the twin rocks above Supai Village. They are variously called the Prince and Princess, God and Goddess, or the petrified remains of two brothers who are said to have led the tribe into Havasu Canyon. The rocks stand guard and preside over the crops of corn, squash, and beans to ensure a good harvest. Legend prophesied that when the rocks fall the village and the tribe will cease to exist.

TOPOCOBA HILLTOP AND SPRING: Topocoba is a Havasupai word for hilltop spring. A spring is at the base of the Coconino Sandstone along the trail into the canyon. A variant name is Topocobya. BGN 1908. (130, 131)

LEE CANYON: This is named for John D. Lee who was rumored to have lived for three years with the Havasupai Indians while hiding from Federal agents after the 1857 Mountain Meadows Massacre. BGN 1932.

RATTLESNAKE CANYON: This is a descriptive term. BGN 1932.

MOUNT SPOONHEAD: This is named for a Havasupai Indian whose head was shaped like a spoon. He carried the U.S. Mail and was involved in constructing a trail in 1902. BGN 1925. (45)

MOUNT BURRO: This was named for Captain Burro, a Havasupai Indian and friend to William W. Bass. It was earlier called Burro Butte. BGN 1925. (45)

WATAHOMIGIE POINT: This is a Havasupai family name (an official BGN spelling) means stripped house. It is sometimes spelled Watahomigi and Warabomegi. BGN 1988. (127, 45)

WESCOGAME POINT: This is a Havasupai family name. BGN 1925. (45)

LONG MESA: This is a descriptive name. BGN 1932.

YUMTHESKA MESA: This is a Havasupai family name. (45)

RL   RM 161
POCKET POINT: This is a descriptive name for the several water pockets located at the rim. Also, it may be named for the term pocket which in Arizona is used to describe small, rounded openings, not exactly canyons, like the unnamed canyon below Pocket Point.

FLATIRON BUTTE: This is a descriptive term.

RR   RM 164.5
TUCKUP CANYON AND POINT: Tuckup is a corruption of Tucket. Mines in the drainage were part of the Tucket Mining District. Variant names are Hundred and Sixtyfour Mile Canyon and Tucket Canyon. BGN 1964.

THE DOME: This is a descriptive name for the isolated butte on the Esplanade.

S B POINT: This may be named as it is a "son of a bitch" to reach.

THE CORK: Origin unknown, but probably a descriptive term for the shape of the butte on the Esplanade.

RL   RM 164.5 to 273.5

HUALAPAI INDIAN RESERVATION: The Hualapai Indian
Reservation is the fourth reservation (along with Paiute, Navajo, and
Havasupai) with land bordering Grand Canyon. Wala Pa'a is the term
given by Garces in 1776 to the entire tribe of Pai Indians. Ives used the
word Hualapai in 1858. Ives employed Yarateva, a Mohave chief to lead
him from the Colorado east along Beale's wagon road. He heard the
term Ja Whala Pa'a (meaning Pine Tree Mountain People) for these
Indians and transcribed it to Hualapai. (34, 45, 54)

RL   RM 166.5

NATIONAL CANYON: Origin unknown. A flurry of mining activity
was centered in National Canyon in 1891. A USGS cableway upstream
of the canyon was the scene of a fatal helicopter accident on Dec. 8,
1983. A chartered helicopter had flown two Bureau of Land Management administrators to compare a remote part of the canyon with another
designated for wilderness status. The helicopter was flying downstream
at an estimated airspeed of 80-100 knots at about 30-50 ft above river
level on the return flight to Las Vegas. Two USGS researchers quickly
left the cable car when they saw the helicopter on a collision path. The
one inch cable caught the engine cowling, then the rotor mast, flipping
the helicopter upside down into the river. The occupants were rescued
by the researchers, but one man died. Due to this accident and others,
a Special Federal Aviation Regulation (SFAR 50-2) became fully
effective in 1988. This regulation established flight free zones below
14,500 ft in 44% of the Park. Other areas have separate minimum
altitudes for tour craft and general aviation aircraft. (143, 152)

RR   RM 168

FERN GLEN: Maidenhair ferns grow in the moist cliffs and seeps
along this shady canyon.

> **ALAMO WINDOW:** Harvey Butchart, famous canyon hiker
> who has explored over 15,000 miles of trails in Grand Canyon,
> calls the arch at Fern Glen, Alamo Window. It is also known as
> Fern Glen Arch. (18)

> **WILLOW CANYON:** A descriptive name.

STAIRWAY CANYON AND FAULT: Origin unknown, but there is a stairstep-like climb out of the canyon. The Mohawk-Stairway fault was named by George Billingsley in 1970, though it was originally named the Stairway-Willow Springs Monocline and Gateway-Stairway fault by John Maxson in 1969. (130)

MOHAWK CANYON: Norman Imùs, a Hualapai Indian, told P.T. Reilly that Mohawk Canyon was called Moko Canyon, a route used by Paiutes and Hualapais to cross the Colorado River when fighting with each other. In the 1890s it was also called Mono, Mohaw, Moho, and Mohawk. Mining activity was at its peak in this canyon in 1898. Spier's 1928 map in his *Havasupai Ethnology* called the canyon Moho, though the Havasupai called the canyon by another name which translates as pine precipice, a place where pinyon nuts were plentiful. On a 1944 USGS map, the canyon was labeled Gateway Canyon, while the next smaller, tributary west and river left was called Mohawk Canyon. (18, 95, 127, 130, 148)

> **GATEWAY RAPIDS:** Origin unknown, but it may be a reference to the gateway or portal between the Hualapai and Havasupai lands to the south and the Paiute lands to the north. A previous name for Mohawk Canyon, now used for the rapids.

COVE CANYON: This is a descriptive name. Big Point Canyon is a variant name.

> **BIG POINT:** This is a descriptive name.

> **BURRO CANYON:** Origin unknown.

RED SLIDE: This is a descriptive name for the zone of extensive landslide debris on river right. The debris of this large scale rotational landslide is derived from the red sandstones of the Supai Group of Formations and the underlying Redwall Limestone. (7, 13)

SADDLE HORSE CANYON: This is named for the spring above.

HONGA SPRING: Honga is a Hualapai family name. (138)

> **McKEE POINT:** Edwin Dinwiddie McKee (1906-1984) was Chief Park Naturalist at Grand Canyon for 11 years, Director of Research at the Museum of Arizona in 1941, Professor of Geology at the University of Arizona in 1942-1952, and geologist with the USGS from 1953-1977. He published many monographs on the Kaibab, Toroweap, Coconino Supai, Redwall, Muav, Bright Angel, and Tapeats formations, as well as the volcanic geology of Grand Canyon. His favorite area in the Grand Canyon was the Esplanade rim. The name was proposed by Joeseph G. Hall, a biologist, in 1986. BGN 1986. (54, 127)

TOROWEAP VALLEY, LAKE, FAULT, AND OVERLOOK: Toroweap is a Paiute word meaning either a gully or a dry wash. It does not mean canyon, valley, or deep gorge. Toro or tono can also mean greasewood, while weap means canyon. In a 1932 letter to the BGN, the Superintendent of the Grand Canyon states, "Near Lee's Ferry there lives an old Paiute Indian whom we know only as 'Joedie' and who told me, through an interpreter that Toroweap means 'Garden Spot in the Canyon.' He also says that the common English pronunciation of this word differs from the Paiute pronunciation and they pronounce the word more nearly as if there were no 'r' in it." A Paiute word toayoweap means Cattail Canyon. A variant name is Torowip or Mukoontuweap. Professor Almon Thompson, of Powell's party, named the valley from the Paiute word Mukoomtuweap meaning straight canyon, as the valley is about 25 miles long. (80, 110, 120, 138)

> **TUWEAP:** An associated name of Toroweap is Tuweap, or Tuweep, from Mukoomtuweap. Tuweap is Paiute for land or earth. Tuweep was the name given the Post Office at the Kent Ranch in Toroweap Valley. John Riffey, Tuweap District Ranger and Toroweap Valley resident from 1938-1980, called his dirt airstrip Tuweap International, from which he flew his plane *Pogo* (short for Pegasus). (1, 7, 80)

> **VULCANS THRONE:** Dutton named Vulcan's Throne, a volcanic cinder cone, in 1882. He wrote, "Apart from the merely scenic effects it would be hard to find anywhere in the

world a spot presenting so much material for the contemplation of the geologist." Vulcan was the Roman god of fire and metal-working. (36)

RC   RM 178

VULCANS ANVIL: C.H. Birdseye, Chief of the 1923 USGS Expedition, called this 60 ft basalt volcanic neck which protrudes from midstream, Lava Rock Island. It has also been called Vulcan's Forge, Nigger Head (this derogatory name is no longer used), and Lava Pinnacle. (10, 28)

RR   RM 179.5

LAVA FALLS AND TRAIL: Frederick Dellenbaugh wrote of Powell's first expedition that, "The canyon appeared to have been once filled by the lava to the depth of fifteen hundred feet. They named the descent Lava Falls and made a portage." Powell wrote, "What a conflict of water and fire there must have been here! Just imagine a river of molten rock running down into a river of melted snow. What a seething and boiling of the waters; what clouds of steam rolled into the heavens!" A 800 to 1,400 ft lava dam once blocked the river and created a lake upstream, possibly the cause of the various levels of waterfalls in Havasu Canyon and the deposits at Red Slide. The river eventually wore through and around the dam. The drop in Lava Falls is 13 ft, though it still deserves the rating of a "10." Lava Falls Trail drops over 2,300 ft from Toroweap Valley. It follows an old Indian trail to what was called Shivwits Crossing, where Indians would cross the Colorado River. (13, 32, 83, 92b)

> **THE EYE OF ODIN:** A small arch or hole in the lava rock above Lava Falls is affectionately called the Eye of Odin by river guides. Odin, the Scandinavian or Viking god of war and the dead, obtained his knowledge from the Well of Wisdom. He begged Mimir, the custodian of the well, for a drink. Mimir said he must pay for it with one of his eyes which Odin then gave him. Odin later passed on the wisdom and the knowledge of the runes or magical inscriptions to mankind. Odin is called Woden by the Anglo-Saxons and Wotan by the Germans. (51)

> **THE COVE:** Origin unknown. Located on the rim, The Cove probably got its name for its protected location.

PROSPECT CANYON AND VALLEY: This canyon was named by John Conners and Franklin French, two prospectors from Holbrook, Arizona. French married Emma Bachelor Lee several years after John D. Lee was executed. Debris from Prospect Canyon (and not a lava ledge) forms the rapid at Lava Falls. (92a)

> **WARM SPRINGS:** This is a descriptive name for the warm springs which flow into the river over the travertine deposits.

> **AUBREY VALLEY AND CLIFFS:** This is named for Francois Xavier Aubrey, the great "Skimmer of the Plains." In 1850, Aubrey road horseback from Santa Fe, New Mexico to Independence, Missouri, on a wager of $1,000 that he could do it in eight days. He finished three hours earlier than the wager, though several horses were killed in the attempt. He then repeated the return ride in even less time. A variant name is Aubry Valley and Cliffs. (4, 45, 102)

HELLS HOLLOW: Origin unknown, but probably a reference to the hot lava rocks making one feel that they are broiling in Hades. A second Hell's Hollow is an arm of Whitmore Canyon.

BEECHER SPRING: Beecher is a Hualapai family name.

UINKARET MOUNTAINS: The following three peaks and 118 volcanic cones were collectively called the Uinkaret Mountains. Powell reported that Uinkaret, meaning pine mountain people, was the tribal name for the Paiute Indians living in this region. Lt. Amiel Whipple first called these the High Mountains in 1854, Lt. Ives named them the North Side Mountains in 1858, and the Mormon pioneers called them the Pine or Sawmill Mountains in reference to the trees cut for the Mormon Temple in St. George, Utah. The three main peaks are surrounded by 118 smaller volcanic cones. (33, 45, 54, 58)

> **MOUNT TRUMBULL:** Powell named the mountain in honor of Illinois Senator Lyman Trumbull (1854-73) in 1870. Mount Trumbull is also the official name of Bundyville, the small, Mormon community on the Arizona Strip. Bundyville was

settled by Abraham Bundy in 1916 after he and his family were forced out of old Mexico by Pancho Villa. It was later abandoned after the Taylor Grazing Law of 1934 restricted use of open range. (27, 45, 110)

MOUNT LOGAN: Named by Powell for General John A. Logan, Senator from Illinois, who was a general in the Civil War. (45, 110)

MOUNT EMMA: Mount Emma was either named by Powell or by Dutton in 1882 for Powell's wife and cousin, Emma Dean. After nine years of marriage, Emma gave birth to a daughter, named Mary Dean, on September 8, 1871, while Powell was in Cataract Canyon on his second expedition. (45, 110)

RL   RM 187.5
HELICOPTER PAD: A helicopter service, operated by Tony Heaton and the Bar Ten Ranch, brings river passengers to and from river trips. It is located above the old high water line on the Hualapai Indian Reservation.

RR   RM 188
WHITMORE CANYON, TRAIL, POINT, AND WASH: This canyon is named for a St. George, Utah man named Whitmore who was a rancher at the base of Mt. Trumbull around 1872 when Dellenbaugh surveyed the area with Dr. Almon H. Thompson. He may have been related to James M. Whitmore who herded cattle and sheep to Pipe Spring, built a dugout in 1863 which can still be seen at Pipe Spring National Monument, and with Robert McIntyre was killed by Indians in January 1866. A variant name is Queantoweap Valley. (33, 45, 127)

WILSON AUSTIN -- SURVEYORS, CASA GRANDE, ARIZ.: This inscription can be seen from the river on the overhang below the trail on river right. Austin and Wilson were dam site surveyors for the Bureau of Reclamation's Prospect Canyon Project in the late 1950s. (132)

MOLLIES NIPPLE: At a height of 5,551 ft, Mollies Nipple is visible from the river upstream of Whitmore Trail. Almon Thompson, Powell's geographer on the 1872 expedition, called it Mollie's Nipple and said it was also known as White Cone.

Nipple describes the appearance, while who Mollie was is a mystery. (1, 44)

HURRICANE FAULT AND CLIFFS: Mormon ranchers called the region Hurricane Hill after an exploring party of Mormon officials were overtaken by a heavy whirlwind, like a hurricane, which blew off the top of the buggy near the present town of Hurricane, Utah. Dellenbaugh writes that the Mormons applied the name Hurricane Ledge to the long line of sharp cliffs along the western boundary of the Uinkaret Plateau. The cliffs are over 2,000 ft high in places. The fault dissects the Arizona Strip and runs from Peach Springs, Arizona to Cedar City, Utah. The Paiute Indians called the Hurricane Cliffs Chunquawakab, meaning a line of cliffs. (33, 80, 110)

RR   RM 193
BOULDER WASH: This is a descriptive name for the numerous boulders in the wash.

RL   RM 194
194 MILE: River runners sometime call this beach Hualapai Acres.

RL/RR   RM 196
FROGY FAULT: In 1981, George Billingsley and Peter Huntoon named this fault after Frog Spring near where the fault crosses Upper Parashant Canyon. (130)

RR   RM 198.5
PARASHANT CANYON: Two meanings are given for Parashant, a Paiute word. It may come from Paria-a-sant meaning tanned elk skin or the softening of an elk hide. The area was a favorite gathering place for the southern Paiute bands after the fall hunting season where they visited, dried their meats, and tanned skins. The word may also mean plenty of water, for there is a spring at the head of the canyon below Poverty Mountain. It was named about 1900. Another spelling is Parashunt, while a local name is Mule Canyon. (4, 80, 138)

In June 1946, Georgie Clark and Harry Aleson floated 76 miles from Parashant Canyon to Emery Falls where they were picked up by a NPS cruiser. The pair used an inflatable Air Force-type rubber raft, life jackets, and swim fins to navigate the 48,000 cfs flow. Georgie (1911-1992), "The Woman of the River," took her first Colorado River swim from about River Mile 218 with Harry in June 1945. Born Georgie de Ross, she married Harold Clark in 1927, then James White after 1935, but she preferred to be called Georgie Clark. However, she was ultimately married to the Colorado River after her first Grand Canyon run in 1952. Georgie pioneered the use of pontoon rafts powered by outboard motors. She took up to 30 Royal River Rats on her G-rig (two 28 ft pontoons tied on either side of a 33 ft pontoon). She ran her last raft trip in 1991. (63)

ANDRUS CANYON AND POINT: In 1866, Captain James Andrus' party killed some Indians whom they suspected killed two white men (Whitmore and McIntyre). But it was later discovered that they were peaceful Paiutes who had traded for the murdered men's clothing. The real criminals were never apprehended. (45, 110)

MOUNT DELLENBAUGH: This 6,750 ft peak was named by Powell for Frederick S. Dellenbaugh, the 17 year old self-taught artist who went on the second expedition in 1871. Dellen-baugh's duty was to sketch a running profile of the river's left wall. He worked as a topographer and later became the expedition's historian by writing the books *The Romance of the Colorado River* in 1902 and *A Canyon Voyage* in 1908. (45)

LONE MOUNTAIN: Origin unknown, but probably a descriptive term for this isolated area.

RR   RM 204
SPRING CANYON: Several springs are to be found in this canyon.

                                                               RM 205.5
KOLB RAPIDS OR 205 MILE RAPIDS: Named for Emery Clifford Kolb (1881-1976), the photographer of Grand Canyon. Emery and his brother Ellsworth started a photographic studio on South Rim in 1903. When water was scarce at the rim, he would hike four miles down with his negatives to the finishing room at Indian Garden. The Kolbs navigated the Colorado River from Wyoming to the Gulf of California in 1911-12. (31, 60)

RR   RM 206.5
INDIAN CANYON: C.H. Birdseye, Chief of the USGS 1923 Expedition named Indian Canyon as "La Rue found several old Indian cliff

dwellings about 1/3 mile up on the right with remnants of pottery, baskets, and arrowheads." Recent relics, called the Bundy Jars, were left by members of the Arizona Strip's ranching Bundy family. (10)

RL   RM 209
GRANITE PARK CANYON AND FAULT: Birdseye also named this canyon. He wrote in his journal for September 27, "At this point the river widens considerably and granite outcrops in the side canyons together with the wide river valley with many willow trees along the left bank led us to call the place 'Granite Park.'" The fault was named by George Billingsley and Peter Huntoon in 1981. One mile below Granite Park, on river left, is a dome, named "the Cathedral" by Robert Stanton in 1890. (10, 94)

RR   RM 211.5
FALL CANYON: Origin unknown. A five meter dune, called a star dune, makes this beach unique. Star dunes are rare in the United States but prevalent in northwest Sonora, Mexico. They are defined as having a central pyramid with three or more radiation arms, each roughly symmetrical in cross-section. A star dune is produced when wind currents come from many angles or from intersecting canyons. (8)

RL   RM 213
PUMPKIN SPRING: A descriptive term, this orange, travertine dome, similar to the Sipapu in the Little Colorado River drainage, is created by spring flow depositing calcium carbonate. Opposite Pumpkin Springs, the remains of an unknown prospector's fire place and tent platform can be seen half way up the slope.

RL   RM 215.5
THREE SPRINGS CANYON: Birdseye named this canyon. He wrote in his journal for September 29, "We called this Three Springs Canyon on account of three flowing springs, one being within 200 yards of the river." An unnamed arch can be seen on the western rim's skyline, opposite the canyon. (10)

                                                                RM 216 to 264
LOWER GRANITE GORGE: Lower Granite Gorge is 50 miles long and stretches from below Three Springs Canyon to Dry Canyon. In 1890, Robert Stanton described the gorge as "A real canyon. River more powerful, the *bad* rapids worse, and the good rapids bad." (94)

TRAIL CANYON: A very faint to non-existent trail to the Snyder Mine goes up this canyon and this may be the origin of the name. Shanley Spring, a pool in a fall in the Upper Redwall is located along the trail. Snyder was the prospector that the Kolb brothers met on their 1911-12 river trip a day's travel below Lava Falls and six miles above Diamond Creek. Snyder had come down Diamond Creek with a burro and a pack mule and was doing some assessment work on some copper claims he reached by crossing the river on a raft. In 1891, Snyder and his son left their home in Vernal, upset their boat in the Canyon of Lodore, and borrowed a horse from the Chew family to escape the river. The main trail to the Snyder Mine is up 214 Mile Canyon. (18, 60)

220 MILE CANYON: Some river guides call this canyon and the camps along the river the Gorilla Camps for the silhouette of the rocks on river left which resembles a gorilla's profile looking upstream.

SIX PACK EDDY: River runners have named this eddy for its collection of flotsam and jetsam, which often includes lost beer.

GRANITE SPRING CANYON: Claude Birdseye named this canyon. He wrote in his journal of October 1, 1923, "...I traversed up a deep canyon from the left to elevation 2,054. Found a small spring in granite gorge of the main fork at elevation 1,940 and called this canyon Granite Spring Canyon." Today, the spring is a minor spring at best. (10)

"Canyon of the Colorado," No. 1633A, W.H. Jackson Photo. & Pub. Co., Denver, Colo.

"Grand Canyon of Arizona fr. O'Neill Point," No 014454, Copyright 1902 Detroit Photographic Co. Note: Photograph taken from Yavapai Point, left to right can be seen Shiva Temple, Isis Temple, Cheops Pyramid, The Colonnade, Buddha Temple, and Manu Temple.

RL   RM 225.5

DIAMOND CREEK AND PEAK: In 1776, the Franciscan Padre Garces first called Diamond Creek the Arroyo de San Alexo. It was rediscovered and named Diamond Creek by Lt. Joseph Christmas Ives and Dr. John S. Newberry, who arrived on April 5, 1858. Newberry was the first geologist to see the Grand Canyon. He identified many fossils and described the rocks near the mouth of Diamond Creek in 1861. F.W. von Egloffstein and H.B. Mollhausen, two artists on the expedition, sketched the first drawings of Grand Canyon at this location. (45, 54, 102)

Why Ives named the drainage Diamond Creek is unknown, but an 1890s traveler noted that "On comparing the mud color of the Colorado with the crystalline purity of this creek, one realizes to what the later might owe its name." Tourists were able to visit the area once a stop of the Atlantic and Pacific Railroad was made at nearby Peach Springs in 1882. They made the 20 mile journey down Peach Springs Wash to its junction with Diamond Creek, two miles from the Colorado River. At the junction, lodging was available at the Farlee Hotel (also known as the Diamond Creek Hotel) which was built by Judge H. Farlee and his partner Young in 1884. The hotel was a single room shanty with an attached kitchen and two bedrooms. It closed in 1920 and later ceased to exist after local ranchers and Indians carried away the lumber piece by piece for other projects. (44, 54, 67, 130)

In October 1894, Charles L. Potter, First Lieutenant of Engineers, U.S. Army and three others rafted from Diamond Creek down for two days, lost their boat while portaging a rapid, then hiked out a bighorn trail to the Railroad. (55)

The pyramid-shaped Diamond Peak is 3,512 ft high. It should not be confused with Diamond Butte, which is west of the Hurricane Cliffs. Dellenbaugh named Diamond Butte because he found a large ant hill covered with small, perfect quartz crystals that sparkled in the sun like diamonds. (45)

In April 1931, Ivan Bundy, then 23 years of age, drowned in the river below Whitmore Wash when he and Floyd Iverson tried to swim across the river. Floyd, Chester Bundy, and another man put-in at Parashant with a 180 pound galvanized boat with air chambers in each end. Their boat tipped over downstream and they lost most of their food and a box of dynamite brought along for fishing. The men reported that at Diamond Creek they saw written the names of Glen and Bessie Hyde and the date November 31, 1928 (sic) on a plank used for tools in the Government Survey blacksmith shop (see Honeymoon Rapid). The men rowed downstream and hiked out at Separation Canyon, never having found Ivan Bundy's body. The hike took five days until they found out that only the east fork was passable. They returned home by following an old road to the Snyder Mine on the Arizona Strip. (27)

> **PEACH SPRINGS CANYON:** Garces passed by here on June 15, 1775 and named the spring Pozos de San Basilio (St. Basil's Wells). Lt. Ives called it New Creek. In 1858, Lt. Beale, who stopped by with his camel entourage, called it Indian Spring. It is not known who named the canyon after peach trees growing by a spring which were found in 1881. They may have been brought to the area by Mormon settlers in 1852. (45)

RL   RM 229 and 230.5
TRAVERTINE CANYON, RAPIDS AND FALLS: Travertine, or calcium carbonate, is dissolved from the upper limestone layers by groundwater and springs and is deposited on the canyon walls. The Falls are below the canyon and rapids.

RM 232
HONEYMOON RAPIDS: It is thought that Glen R. and Bessie Haley Hyde, the Honeymoon Couple, perished at 232 Mile Rapid when they were thrown from their sweep scow boat. They started their river trip from Green River, Utah on October 20, 1928, six months after their wedding. Stopping at Bright Angel Creek, the couple hiked out to visit Emery Kolb who offered them life jackets which Glen refused. When they did not arrive at Needles on the appointed date, Glen's father became alarmed. A search party led by the Kolb brothers found the upright boat below Mile 237 with the bow line caught below water on Christmas Day. Their possessions were on the boat but there was no sign of the couple. Bessie's diary said they passed Lava Falls on Nov. 27, and the last entry was dated Nov. 30. The mystery of the Honeymoon Couple has not been solved. Had Bessie completed the trip, she would have been the first woman through the Grand Canyon. (63)

BRIDGE CANYON: Birdseye camped at the mouth of what he called Natural Bridge Canyon. He stated that, "This canyon was so named by reason of a small natural bridge a third mile up from the river." Below the canyon at River Mile 237.5 is the location of the proposed hydroelectric dam, variously called Bridge Canyon Dam or Hualapai Dam, whose proponents said would prevent the silting up of Lake Mead. If built, the 700 ft dam could have backed up water to Kanab Creek. (10)

The story of Jim Ervin is linked to Bridge Canyon. In 1931, Jim and his partner were trying to get jobs at Boulder Dam (later called Hoover Dam), which was under construction. They got tired of being thrown off freight trains on their route west, so they decided to walk down Peach Springs Wash and float to the construction site. At Diamond Creek they found an abandoned boat and set off downstream. The boat flipped and to avoid what they soon realized to be a suicidal trip, they stopped near River Mile 234. Ervin climbed out of the canyon for help. The search party was able to get down Bridge Canyon, then hike up river. But Ervin's partner was never found. Sheriff's deputies called the route that Ervin said he used through the Redwall to be impossible. But Bill Belknap and John Evans later climbed the route without undue difficulty. (18, 131)

GNEISS CANYON: Gneiss is a course grained metamorphic rock with variable mineral composition in a banded texture. Feldspar is usually abundant, but other common minerals include quartz, amphibole, garnet, and mica. Rapids below this canyon have been drowned by the waters of Lake Mead.

SEPARATION CANYON AND RAPIDS: Dellenbaugh said that the Professor, Almon Harris Thompson, called the rapid Catastrophe Rapid, but it has since been called Separation Rapid. It was here that Oramel G. Howland, his brother Seneca, and William H. Dunn separated from Powell's first expedition on August 28, 1869. Disagreements and the worst rapid of the expedition are thought to have made their decision. The men hiked out Separation Canyon to the Shivwits Plateau and were never seen again. Powell learned from Chuarrumpeak, the Kaibab Paiute chief, that his people killed three white miners whom they thought had killed a Hualapai woman on the south side of the river. Whether these three miners were Powell's men has never been verified. (45, 83)

Robert Stanton felt that the plaque on Powell Monument at South Rim should be replaced with one which included all the names of the men who accompanied Powell on his two expeditions. His book, *Colorado River Controversies*, with a forward by Julius Stone, outlines his convictions. Russell Frazier, Willis Johnson, Julius Stone, and Stone's son placed the first plaque to partially right this wrong on the granite wall at Separation Canyon in 1934. The plaque was replaced in 1943 when waters of Lake Mead covered up the cenotaph. (21, 63)

RL   RM 246

SPENCER CANYON: This is named after Charles or Charley Spencer (1840-1886), an army scout, friend of the Hualapai Indians, prospector, rancher, and miner. He married a Hualapai woman and was called a squaw man. He was one of General George Crook's scouts in 1872-73 and a guide for the Wheeler Expedition of 1871 which surveyed northern Arizona. He served as an interpreter and was active in helping to establish the Hualapai Indian Reservation. He is credited with finding a silver lode in Havasu Canyon in 1873 and with Dan O'Leary reported a silver mine near the mouth of the Little Colorado River in 1877. When the Hualapai Reserve was set aside in 1883, he built a stone cabin in Meriwhitica Canyon and claimed two of the finest springs in the area. He built irrigation ditches and cultivated land where he planted vegetables and a peach orchard. The area was called Indian Gardens, not to be confused with the place by the same name along the Bright Angel Trail. He later moved to Milkweed Canyon and had a ranch house on top of the mesa which was called the Spencer Ranch. He was partners with a man called Cohan, but separated after a serious quarrel over livestock. They had another quarrel about an acre of land and Cohan killed Spencer in Truxton Canyon. The two prominent Redwall Limestone buttes on the skyline at Spencer Canyon are sometimes called the Spencer Towers or the Spencer Bells, a descriptive name for the shapes. (45, 67, 145)

> **LAVA CLIFF RAPIDS:** Powell described this rapid as having a bold, lava-capped escarpment at the beginning of the rapid on the right side. The rapid earned the reputation as being one of the most fearful rapids in the Grand Canyon. On the left, Spencer Canyon added boulders to choke the river and on the right, a hundred foot wall of granite was topped by fifty more feet of jagged lava, the top of which can still be seen today. Birdseye says Stone was first to call this Bold Escarpment Rapids during his 1909 trip. Ellsworth Kolb called this the Last Portage

as it was the last and 14th portage of the Kolb's 1911-1912 trip. (10, 60, 83)

MERIWHITICA CANYON, SPRING, AND FAULT: Meriwhitica comes from a Hualapai word (variously spelled) meaning hard dirt or hard ground, due to the character of the soil in the canyon. The soil and a 500 ft cliff in the canyon are derived from travertine deposits. Matavila, the Hualapai Indian Creator god, lived alone and one day decided to create humans. He cut canes growing in the water and prayed for each tribe to come to life. He journeyed east and took up residence in Whahavo, a cave in Meriwhitica Canyon. (4, 34, 45)

The canyon was formerly used by the Hualapai Indians as a permanent camp. In 1921 or 1924, a meteor crashed into the north wall of Milkweed Canyon across from the village, leaving a scar on the Redwall Limestone cliff. Believing this to be a bad omen, the Hualapais abandoned the village. (145)

MILKWEED CANYON AND SPRING: The abundant milkweeds which grow along the creek are probably the source of the name. Charles Spencer claimed ownership of the spring in early 1881 . (45)

HINDU CANYON: Origin unknown, but possibly named after the native race and religion of India. An example of stream capture or stream piracy is taking place at a tributary to Hindu Canyon where the drainage is in the process of being captured or drained by Bridge Canyon. (145)

RR   RM 248.5
SURPRISE CANYON: Origin unknown. Birdseye called this canyon Bottle Neck Canyon on account of the exceedingly narrow entrance where it joins the Colorado River and the deep wide valley above. He found fresh cattle tracks within a quarter of a mile of the river and a small amount of clear water. The canyon's two arms are Green Spring Canyon (to the east) and the Twin Spring Canyon (to the west). (10, 130)

RL   RM 249
CLAY TANK CANYON AND LOST CREEK RAPIDS: Origins unknown. The canyon is sometimes called Lost Tank Basin. It is

erroneously reported that the origin of this name is from an important mining camp, which was rediscovered in 1906. The camp, located elsewhere in Mohave County, was located in a small basin surrounded by low hills. (45)

RL   RM 252.5
REFERENCE POINT CREEK OR MAXSON CANYON: The origin of Reference Point Creek is unknown, but it probably stems from an old survey point used by topographers. In 1969, Buzz Belknap named the canyon for John H. Maxson, a geologist who studied and named the early proterozoic Zoroaster Granite and Brahma Schist rocks. The canyon's tributary is called Horse Flat Canyon. (7, 73, 130)

RR   RM 255.5
SALT CREEK AND DEVILS SLIDE RAPIDS: Salt Creek is a descriptive name in reference to the salty taste of the water in a spring a half mile up from the Colorado River. Frank Brown of the USGS named Devils Slide Rapids in 1935.

RL   RM 257
JACKSON CANYON AND TRIUMPHAL ARCH RAPIDS: Buzz Belknap named Jackson Canyon in 1969. Who Jackson was is unknown. The rapid was named for Triumphal Arch which can be seen above the river. The 100 ft arch was named after the successful completion of the mapping survey by the 1923 USGS Birdseye party. (7, 131)

RR   RM 259.5
BURNT SPRING CANYON, POINT, AND SPRING AND WATER-FALL RAPIDS: The canyon was renamed in 1973 by local use of the name Burnt Springs, located in the drainage. It is also known as Burnt Canyon, most likely from the mescal pits near the spring where the ground is burnt. Mescal, also called Century Plant or Agave, was collected by Indians and the fleshy emerging stalk baked in earthen pits for food. Waterfall was a descriptive name for the rapid now underwater. (130)

RL   RM 260
QUARTERMASTER CANYON: This canyon is named for Quartermaster, a Hualapai Indian who lived here about 1900-1930. In the army, a quartermaster is an officer in charge of providing quarters, clothing, fuel, and transportation for troops. The 1962 Jones roll map labels this

site as Cass Monument and Flour Sack Rapid, origins of which are unknown. (45)

Aleson's Cave is located in the cliff of travertine between the arms of Quartermaster Canyon. Harry Leroy Aleson (1899-1972) hoped to create a modern cliff dwelling which he called MY HOME by glassing the entrance. Bill Belknap reported fig trees and travertine lined irrigation ditches near the cave. The ditches were left by the Hualapai Indians who lived and farmed the flats long ago. Aleson was a teen-age aviator in World War I, worked for geophysical firms exploring oil in the Southwest, and was an avid river runner and explorer. He introduced Georgie Clark to river running while lecturing on his upriver expedition at a Sierra Club meeting in 1944. He operated the Larabee & Aleson Western River Tours in Glen Canyon from 1944 into the 1960s, until the waters of Lake Powell drowned many of the sites and self-guided charter boats became available at several marinas. (63)

RM 262

WARDS CAVE RAPIDS: Origin unknown.

RR   RM 263.5
TINCANEBITTS CANYON, POINT, AND SPRING: Origin unknown, it may be a Paiute word. Variant names are Tincanuts and Tincanibus. (27)

RR   RM 264.5
DRY CANYON: Yet another descriptive name for a waterless canyon. The rapid below was called Hell Diver Rapid on the 1962 Jones roll map. (152)5

RR   RM 266
BAT CAVE: In the late-1940's to early-1950's, the U.S. Guano Corporation mined bat guano or feces on a commercial scale for plant fertilizer. The dry guano was broken loose by hoes and rakes, then vacuum pumped to loading bins and cages. A tram trolley lifted up to 3,450 pounds of the "ore" along 10,200 ft of cable up to Quartermaster Point on the west rim, 2,600 ft above. It was then trucked to Kingman. The guano was mined out by the early 1960s and abandoned. Remains of a cable transporting system and towers can be seen on both sides of the river. The cable was cut by a a jet aircraft from Nellis Air Force Base in 1962, the pilot losing eight inches of the wing tip. Today, less expensive nitrate fertilizers are used instead of guano. (6, 130)

EVANS HEAVEN: Springs flowing over the rocks have created this heavenly, shaded nook filled with ferns and Velvet Ash trees. Sometimes difficult to reach, it is a haven from the burning summer sun. It was named by paleobiologist Paul Martin, for Willis Evans, a Paiute Indian. A junior foreman in the NPS, Evans discovered Rampart Cave in the summer of 1936. (139, 140)

WEEPING CLIFFS: Origin unknown, probably a descriptive name for travertine springs dripping over the rock.

MUAV CAVE: A descriptive name for the Muav Limestone. The cave was used by prehistoric sloths and later by Indians. Muav means divide or pass in Paiute.

CAVE CANYON AND COLUMBINE FALLS: This is named for numerous caves in the four mile length. Columbine Falls is named for the flowers which cover both sides of the waterfall. In 1945, this name was suggested by Edward Schenk, Bureau of Mines and Dr. Elzada Clover of the University of Michigan. Elzada Clover and Lois Jotter were the first women to travel the full length of the Colorado River with Norman Nevills in 1938. (23, 45, 127)

Variant names are Emery Falls Canyon and Emery Falls, the origin of which there are two versions. The most credible story is that it is named for Merle "Pop" Emery, a river ferryman who lived nearby and who discovered the Bat Cave in the early 1930s. Other information states that Emery Kolb named the falls after himself and had some local support, but the name was not officially accepted as he was still alive at the time. (127, 130)

> **RAMPART CAVE AND FAULT:** The name Rampart Cave, has been in use since 1936 when it was discovered by Willis Evans, a Paiute Indian working for the NPS as a foreman of a CCC Camp at Pearce Ferry. The name was submitted to BGN by the Bureau of Mines. A rampart is a wide bank of earth, often with a wall on top, built around a fort to help defend it. In the cave were discovered the remains of the extinct, giant, Shasta ground sloth. A sixty inch dung profile showed that

sloths inhabited the cave for 25,000 years. Rampart Cave also contained an abundance of Late Pleistocene (14,000 to 35,000 years ago) biological remains, including desert tortoise, lizards, birds, marmots, rabbit, ringtailed cat, puma, lynx, mountain goat, mountain sheep, and horse. Packrat middens and pollen also give evidence for a mixture of woodland and hot desert plant species 30,000 years ago. A steel gate was installed to prevent vandalism and to preserve the remains, but sadly, the deposits caught on fire in 1976 when someone forced an entrance. Priceless paleontological remains were lost. Rampart Fault was named by Peter Huntoon and George Billingsley in 1982. BGN 1948 (69, 127, 130)

VULTURE CANYON AND CAVE: Unnamed on most maps, this small canyon was named by paleontologists who found a mummified vulture and other Pleistocene remains in a small cave in 1974. The researchers first sighted the cave by seeing vultures fly into it. Arthur Phillips proposed the name in 1975, but it was not approved upon recommendation of the NPS in 1978. (127, 141)

RR   RM 268
TRAVERTINE CLEFT: A descriptive name.

RR   RM 275.5
TRAVERTINE BLUFF: Another descriptive name.

RL/RR   RM 276.5 to Hoover Dam
LAKE MEAD NATIONAL RECREATION AREA: Lake Mead National Recreation Area was established in 1936 and contains more than 3,000 square miles in Arizona and Nevada. Boating, fishing, sailing, water skiing, swimming, hunting, camping, and hiking draw recreationists. (126)

RL/RR   RM 277
GRAND WASH AND CLIFFS: This area was called the Grand Wash in 1875 by surveyors of the Southern Continental Railroad. Grand Wash is a valley formed where the horizontal strata are downfaulted approximately 16,000 ft. It is here that the Colorado River leaves the Grand Canyon. The Grand Wash Cliffs mark the western boundary of the Colorado Plateau and the eastern boundary of the Basin and Range Province. The cliffs are 277 miles downstream from Lee's Ferry and

1,000 miles downstream from Green River, Wyoming. Robert Stanton called the cliffs the Southern Gateway on his 1890 survey expedition. (45, 94)

> **PAIUTE POINT:** This is named after the Paiute Indians who lived in the area.

RL   RM 279
SCORPION ISLAND: This island probably received its name when the waters of Lake Mead, backing up behind Hoover Dam, concentrated and isolated the scorpions of the region on its shores. As the beaches along the Colorado River are eroded from Grand Canyon by the controlled flows from Glen Canyon Dam, sediment is deposited in Lake Mead. Low flows, mud flats, and vegetation make it next to impossible to reach Scorpion Island.

RL   RM 280
PEARCE FERRY: Pearce Ferry is named for Harrison Pearce (born 1818) who was sent by the Mormon Church in 1876 to operate the ferry at this site. The ferry was used until 1883 and Robert Stanton found it abandoned in 1890. Pearce called the ferry Colorado Crossing. The actual ferry site was first discovered in 1862 by Jacob Hamblin during the first recorded circuit around the Grand Canyon. Hamblin was sent to northern Arizona by Brigham Young and the Mormon Church. Pearce and his son James built a stone building, known as Fort Pearce, which was used by the Mormons in defense against the Shivwits and Uinkaret tribes of the Paiute Indians. It is now under the waters of Lake Mead. The spelling of Pearce Ferry is often incorrectly spelled Pierce Ferry. Hamblin used Pierce in a narrative published in 1881 and apparently started the long-standing error, later continued on maps. (45, 94, 115)

RL   RM 280
GRAPEVINE WASH AND MESA: The wash is named for grapevines which grow in a marshy area in the creek bed. (45)

RR   RM 280
PEARCE CANYON: See Pearce Ferry.

RR   RM 281
SNAP CANYON AND POINT: Origin unknown. (49)

RL   RM 283

BADGER COVE: Origin unknown. Badgers are generally found at higher altitudes where they feed on wood rats, squirrels, gophers, prairie dogs, rabbits, insects, and snakes. (52)

RL   RM 283

WHEELER RIDGE: Wheeler Ridge is bisected by the Colorado River. It honors Lt. George M. Wheeler, who was ordered by the War Department in 1871 to conduct a topographic survey of the Southwest called the United States Geographic Surveys West of the One Hundredth Meridian. In October of that year, Wheeler traveled 200 miles up the Colorado River from Camp Mohave (near Needles, California) to Diamond Creek in 33 days. Mohave Indians poled, rowed, and dragged three boats up the fearsome rapids. The expedition was photographed by Timothy H. O'Sullivan, who is credited with being the first photographer of the Grand Canyon. A major fault, called the Wheeler Fault, forms the ridge. (5, 54)

RR   RM 283

COCKSCOMB: A descriptive name for the ridge which resembles the fleshy, red part on the head of a rooster.

RR   RM 283

GODS POCKET: Origin unknown. (49)

RR   RM 287

BOUNDARY POINT: This is near the stateline between Arizona and Nevada, hence the name.

RR   RM 287.5

DRIFTWOOD COVE: This is a descriptive name for the driftwood which was common when debris washed down the Colorado River and met the still waters of Lake Mead. The driftwood log jams, up to 300-400 yards long and dozens of feet thick, often choked the river. The Mexican Hat Expedition of 1940 coined the term DWB (for Driftwood Burner) for anyone who could set a pile of driftwood on fire with one match. (63, 130)

RC and RL   RM 287-290

ICEBERG CANYON AND RIDGE: This was named by Lt. George M. Wheeler in 1871 for the iceberg shape of its northern walls. Iceberg Fault forms the canyon. (45, 130)

RR   RM 287-290

AZURE RIDGE: Origin unknown, but may be a reference to the color of the ridge at sunset. The 1962 Jones roll map calls this the Indian Hills. (145, 152)

RR   RM 291

DEVILS COVE: Origin unknown, but probably a whimsical term for the area next to Hells Kitchen. (49)

RL   RM 295

SOUTH COVE: This cove is on the south side of the Sandy Point promontory, another descriptive name. (131)

> **MEADVIEW:** This residential, retirement community on Grapevine Mesa is located south of Pearce Ferry and South Cove. It has a view to Lake Mead to the west. (126)

RC   RM 300

HUALAPAI ISLANDS: The islands honor the Hualapai Indians.

RM 303-305

VIRGIN CANYON: Origin unknown.

RL   RM 306

GREGGS HIDEOUT: Origin unknown.

RL   RM 307

TEMPLE MESA: This is named for Temple Bar, see below.

RL   RM 312

TEMPLE BAR: Daniel Bonelli named Temple Bar, an early mining camp, for the large, offshore monolith just upstream, called Temple Mesa, which he thought resembled the Mormon Temple in Salt Lake City. Robert Stanton called the mesa the Citadel in 1890. (45, 94)

RM 236 to Hoover Dam

LAKE MEAD: Lake Mead was created when Hoover Dam was completed in 1936. The Boulder Canyon Project Act of 1928 authorized the building of the dam which was to be built in Boulder Canyon. Instead it was built in Black Canyon. In 1947, the name was changed to Hoover Dam to honor ex-president Herbert Hoover. The 726 ft high dam is the highest dam in the western hemisphere. Lake Mead was filled in 1941. It can pool upriver to Gneiss Canyon (RM 236) at an elevation of 1,225 ft. Lake Mead honors Dr. Elwood Mead, Commissioner of Reclamation from 1924-1936. It has a storage capacity of almost 30 million acre feet. (45)

"Grand Canon of Colorado," No. 4929, W.H. Jackson Photo. & Pub. Co., Denver, Colo.

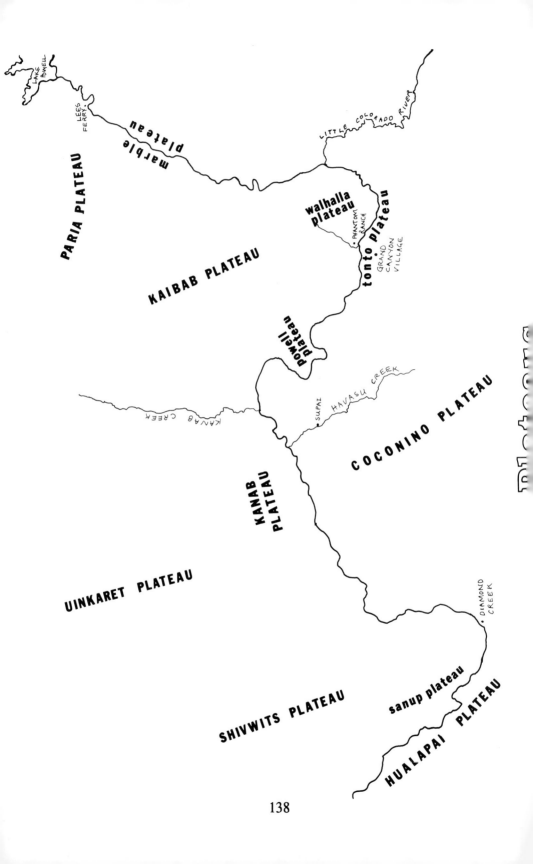

COCONINO PLATEAU: Coconino or Kohonino is the name the Hopi Indians called the Havasupai Indians, later altered to Cosninas by the Spaniards. The Zunis called the Havasupais the Kuhnikwe and the region they inhabit the Kuhni. In 1851, Captain Lorenzo Sitgreaves, who led an expedition across northern Arizona to locate a wagon road for California bound emigrants, called the Havasupais the Cosninos. Lt. Ives called them the Yampais. Coconino Plateau is the area south of the Grand Canyon. It is bordered on the east by the Little Colorado River valley and on the west by the Hualapai Plateau. Variant names include Arizona Plateau, Coanini Plateau, Colorado Plateau, Plateau of Arizona, San Francisco Plateau. BGN 1906. (45)

ESPLANADE: Clarence E. Dutton named the Esplanade in 1882. The word is derived from two Latin words meanin an open, level space between a fortress and a town, or a level space used for public walks and drives. It aptly describes the bare rock expanse on top of the Supai Group west of the Grand Scenic Divide. (36)

HUALAPAI PLATEAU: The Hualapai Plateau is named for the Hualapai Indians. In 1776, Garces called the entire tribe of Pai Indians the Wala Pa'a. Ives used the term Hualapai in 1858 after he heard the term Ja Whala Pa'a, meaning pine tree mountain people. On the north, the Hualapai reservation borders the Colorado River from about River Mile 164 to 273, then extends south in a chevron shape to Route 66. It is bordered on the east by the Coconino Plateau and on the west by the Grand Wash Cliffs.

KAIBAB PLATEAU: Major Powell wrote that Paiute Indians living on the plateau north of Grand Canyon called the area Kaivavwi (kaiuw means mountain and avwi means lying down) and the forests on the plateau the Kaibabits. The word was phonetically rendered to Kaibab in English. However, this term was actually the name the Indians called themselves as they called the plateau Bucksin, their word for deer. This Paiute word was altered by early settlers to Buckskin, a word close in meaning, if not in spelling. Dellenbaugh assumed that the Kaibab, then called Buckskin Mountain, must have received this name from its resemblance to a buckskin stretched out on the ground. The Kaibab Plateau is bounded by the East Kaibab Monocline, the Muav and Big Springs Faults, the Vermilion Cliffs, and the Grand Canyon. (32, 45)

KANAB PLATEAU: Major Powell named Kanab Plateau in 1882. Major Dutton named the area drained by the creek the Kanab Desert. Kanab means willows in Paiute. The Kanab Plateau is bounded on the east by the Muav and Big Springs Faults, on the west by the Toroweap and Sevier Faults, on the north by the Triassic escarpment, and on the south by the Grand Canyon Rim. (36, 83, 130)

MARBLE PLATEAU: Marble Plateau, sometimes called Marble Platform, receives its name from Marble Canyon or Gorge. Major Powell named Marble Canyon for the spectacular grey Redwall Limestone which is painted red by the iron oxide wash from the upper layers. The Redwall Limestone when exposed at river level is polished by the Colorado River and resembles marble, a metamorphosed limestone. (45)

PARIA PLATEAU: Paria is a Paiute word for elk water or for dirty water. (45)

POWELL PLATEAU: Major Clarence Dutton named Powell Plateau in 1882 to honor John Wesley Powell (1834-1902) who led the first two expeditions down the Colorado River: the first from May 24, to Aug 31, 1869 from Green River City, Wyoming to the Virgin River, Nevada and the second from Green River to Paria River (1871) and from Paria to Kanab Creek (1872). Powell was also the Chief of the Rocky Mountain Region Survey (1870-79), first Director of the Bureau of American Ethnology (1879), and the second Director of the USGS (1881-84). The name was placed on a 1921 USGS map. Powell, who had lost his right arm in the Battle of Shiloh, was called Kapurats, a Ute and Shoshone word meaning arm off. BGN 1932. (5, 45, 83)

SANUP PLATEAU: Origin unknown. In Massachusetts, this is an Indian word for a married man. The Sanup Plateau is on the north side of the Colorado River only. It is located between Hidden Canyon and Whitmore Canyon, and is formed by the Espanade Sandstone. (45, 130)

SHIVWITS PLATEAU: Shivwits is a Paiute word meaning either whitish earth or coyote spring from the word Shinabitys Spitz. The Shivwits Plateau is bounded on the east by the Hurricane Fault, on the west by the Grand Wash Fault, the escarpment south of St. George, Utah and the Grand Canyon. (4, 45)

TONTO PLATEAU: Tonto Plateau is named for the Apaches, one of the Tonto Basin Indians. Tonto is the Spanish word for fool. The term was used erroneously because of their supposed foolishness. In the 1800s, the name Tonto Apache was applied to all of the Indians between the White Mountains and the Colorado River. However, this included members of at least two linguistic families and is not applicable to a certain tribe. BGN 1906. (45)

UINKARET PLATEAU: Major Powell named the plateau. In his account of September 20, 1869, he wrote, "For several days we have been discussing the relative merits of several names for these mountains. The Indians call them Uinkarets, the region of pines, and we adopt the name." Uinkaret is a Southern Paiute word meaning pine mountain people or place of the pines. Powell also called them the Wonsits Plateau as the Paiutes also called it Wonsits Tiravu, or Wonsits, their word for antelope. Early white settlers also called it Antelope Plains as great antelope herds existed here during the late 1800s. The Uinkaret Plateau is bounded on the east by the Toroweap and Sevier Faults, on the west by the Hurricane Fault, on the north by the Triassic escarpment, and on the south by the Grand Canyon Rim. (33, 45, 54, 58, 83)

WALHALLA PLATEAU: Walhalla (or Valhalla) is the great hall of the Scandinavian gods, where the god Odin received the souls of the slain Viking warriors and heros. The plateau was named by Francois Matthes in 1906. Earlier, it was called Greenland Point by Mormon settlers who grazed cattle in the vicinity. In 1925, Matthes suggested that the spring and plateau be changed to Greenland as it had pre-existing use prior to 1902. BGN 1906. (44)

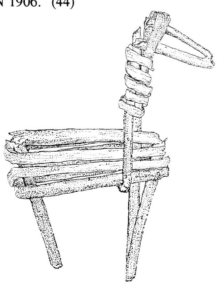

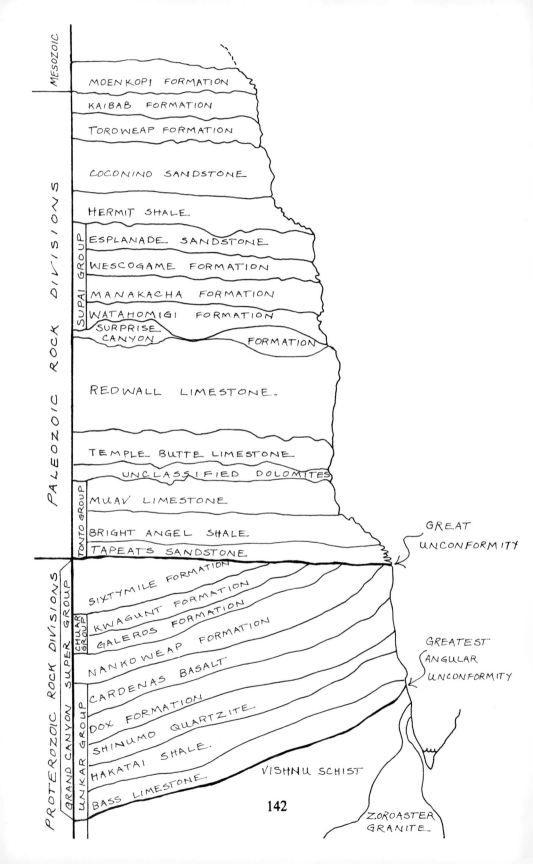

MESOZOIC

PALEOZOIC ROCK DIVISIONS

MOENKOPI FORMATION

KAIBAB FORMATION

TOROWEAP FORMATION

COCONINO SANDSTONE

HERMIT SHALE

SUPAI GROUP

ESPLANADE SANDSTONE

WESCOGAME FORMATION

MANAKACHA FORMATION

WATAHOMIGI FORMATION

SURPRISE CANYON FORMATION

REDWALL LIMESTONE

TEMPLE BUTTE LIMESTONE

UNCLASSIFIED DOLOMITES

TONTO GROUP

MUAV LIMESTONE

BRIGHT ANGEL SHALE

TAPEATS SANDSTONE

GREAT UNCONFORMITY

PROTEROZOIC ROCK DIVISIONS

GRAND CANYON SUPER GROUP

CHUAR GROUP

SIXTYMILE FORMATION

KWAGUNT FORMATION

GALEROS FORMATION

UNKAR GROUP

NANKOWEAP FORMATION

CARDENAS BASALT

DOX FORMATION

SHINUMO QUARTZITE

HAKATAI SHALE

BASS LIMESTONE

VISHNU SCHIST

GREATEST ANGULAR UNCONFORMITY

ZOROASTER GRANITE

142

Mesozoic, Paleozoic, and Precambrian rock formations in and around Grand Canyon have been named by the geologists who studied them. The first presence of a rock group at river level is noted in the upper right margin, however not all can be seen from the river. (13, 48, 49, 59, 66, 71, 73, 82, 109, 145)

Trying to remember the rock layers from the youngest to oldest is difficult for many people. A funny, mnemonic phrase which takes the first letter of each layer and makes a phrase can help. A phrase to remember the sequence of Mesozoic age rocks above Lee's Ferry is, "No kissing my cheeks, silly man!" for Navajo-Kayenta-Moenave-Chinle-Shinarump-Moenkopi.

THE MESOZOIC ROCK DIVISIONS:

NAVAJO SANDSTONE FORMATION: The Navajo Sandstone was named by H.E. Gregory in 1915 as it is widely displayed on the Navajo Reservation, where the type locality is Navajo Canyon. Navajo (or navaju) is an Tewa Indian word meaning place of large plantings. It refers to the large areas of cultivated land developed by the Navajo Indians. An alternative meaning is that it comes from the Spanish word navaja meaning a clasp knife or razor, in reference to the Indian's keenness in trade with the Spanish. The Navajo call themselves Dineh, meaning the people. (45)

KAYENTA FORMATION: The Kayenta Formation was named by A.A. Baker, C.H. Dane, and E.T. McKnight in 1931. The type locality is one mile north of Kayenta, Arizona. Kayenta is the anglicization of the Navajo Indian word tyende meaning where the spring comes out of the side of a hill, or bottomless spring. A variation on the meaning of the name states it to be a natural game pit in describing a spring near this community on the Navajo Indian Reservation which is surrounded by a glue-like clay soil which traps livestock when wet. (45)

MOENAVE FORMATION: The Moenave Formation was named by G.A. Williams in 1954. The type locality is near Moenave, about six miles west of Tuba City, Arizona. There are two members of the Moenave Formation, the upper Springdale Sandstone Member and the basal Dinosaur Canyon Sandstone Member. Moenave (also spelled Moe Ave, Moa Ave, Moen Abi, and Moehavi) was the small settlement visited by Garces in 1776. In 1871, Jacob Hamblin founded a Mormon colony and later traded it to John D. Lee in return for Jacob Pools, Lee's outpost ranch in House Rock Valley where Lee's sixth wife Rachel lived. (14, 45)

RM 0

CHINLE FORMATION: The Chinle Formation was named by H.E. Gregory in 1915. The type locality is Chinle Valley, in northeastern Arizona. Chinle is the corrupted spelling of the Navajo words ch'inlih, meaning at the mouth of the canyon or ichinili meaning where the water comes out. It describes the mouth of Canyon de Chelly where a trading post is located. The Chinle Formation is Triassic in age. (45)

> **OWL ROCK MEMBER:** This is the upper member of the Chinle Formation. Owl Rock is located in Monument Valley.

> **PETRIFIED FOREST MEMBER:** This is the middle unit of the Chinle Formation. The Petrified Forest was first described by Lt. Lorenzo Sitgreaves in 1851. It contains the fossilized remains of 150 million year old trees which have been turned to agate and carnelian by mineral laden waters.

RM 0

> **SHINARUMP MEMBER:** The basal Shinarump Member of the Chinle Formation was named by G.K. Gilbert in 1875 for the Shinarump Cliffs, south of the Vermilion Cliffs in the southern part of Kane County, Utah. Julius F. Stone, in discussing the Shinarump member conglomerate, states that, "Sometimes trunks of trees of considerable size, thoroughly salicified, are found, to which the Paiute Indians have given the name Shinarump, meaning the weapons of Shinav, their wolf god." (98)

RM 0.3

MOENKOPI FORMATION: The Moenkopi Formation was named by L.F. Ward in 1901 for Moenkopi Wash, a tributary to the Little Colorado River. Moenkopi is a Hopi word meaning place of the running water or many springs. A Hopi village by this name was founded by Tuba, chief of Old Oraibi. The Moenkopi Formation is Triassic in age. (45)

THE PALEOZOIC ROCK DIVISIONS:

Two mnemonic phrases to help you remember the sequence of the principle and most obvious Paleozoic rock layers are, "Know the canyon's history, see rocks made by time" for Kaibab - Toroweap - Coconino - Hermit Shale - Supai - Redwall - Muav - Bright Angel - Tapeats. Another phrase which includes the Precambrian schist is "Kissing takes concentration, however, some require more booze to succeed."

RM 0.8

KAIBAB FORMATION: The Kaibab Formation which caps the Kaibab Plateau was first described by N.H. Darton in 1910. The type section was established by Levi Noble in 1928 at Kaibab Gulch near the town of Paria, Utah, six miles north of the Arizona border. Kaibab is the anglicization for the Paiute word kaivavwi meaning mountain lying down. Kaibab is the youngest Permian rock in Grand Canyon. (45)

> **HARRISBURG MEMBER:** This member was first called the Harrisburg Gypsiferous Member by Reeside and Bassler in 1922, then formally named by James Sorauf and George Billingsley in 1991. The type locality is the Harrisburg Dome in southwestern Utah, named for Moses Harris, a Mormon pioneer who settled the area in 1859. (130)

> **FOSSIL MOUNTAIN MEMBER:** Eddie McKee suggest the name Fossil Mountain Member and later formally applied by James Sorauf and George Billingsley in 1991. The type locality is Fossil Mountain, located on the South Rim between Havasupai Point and Bass Camp. (130)

RM 2.1

TOROWEAP FORMATION: The Toroweap Formation was named by Edwin McKee in 1938. The type locality is the eastern wall of Tuweap (now Toroweap) Valley, about eight miles north of the Colorado River. The three members were formally named by James Sorauf and George Billingsley in 1991. Toroweap is a Paiute word meaning variously a gully or a dry wash. Toro or tono can also mean greasewood, while weap means canyon. The Toroweap is of Permian age. (80, 110)

> **WOODS RANCH MEMBER:** The type locality is the Woods Ranch in Whitmore Canyon, west of Mount Emma. Irvin Wood

and his family homesteaded the Mount Trumbull area in the early 1900s. (27, 130)

BRADY CANYON MEMBER: The type locality is Brady Canyon in the same area as the Toroweap Formation. The canyon was named after a local settler. (130)

SELIGMAN MEMBER: The type locality is near Seligman, Arizona. The town was named for the Seligman brothers, who were New York bankers, owners of the Hash Knife Cattle Company, and connected with the A. & P. Railroad (later reorganized in May 1897 as the Santa Fe Railroad). (45, 130)

RM 4.5

COCONINO SANDSTONE: The Coconino Sandstone was named by N.H. Darton in 1910 for the fact that it underlies the Coconino Plateau. The type locality is the Aubrey Cliffs in Coconino County. Coconino is from the Hopi word kohonino, once applied to the Havasupai Tribe. It is also listed as a Havasupai word meaning little water. Robert Brewster Stanton called it the beaded sandstone during his 1890 railroad survey expedition. The Coconino is also Permian in age. (45, 94)

RM 4.9

HERMIT SHALE: The Hermit Shale was named by Levi F. Noble in 1922. The type locality is Hermit Basin at the head of Hermit Canyon. The hermit of Grand Canyon was Louis Boucher. The Hermit Shale is also Permian in age. (45)

RM 11.4

SUPAI GROUP: Originally called the Supai Formation, the Supai Group was first described by N.H. Darton in 1910. The type locality is Supai Village in Havasu Canyon. Supai is shortened from the word Havasupai and means people. When Darton described the Supai, he included the Hermit Shale. The Supai Group was named by Edwin McKee in 1975 and is mostly Pennsylvanian in age. (45, 130)

RM 11.4

ESPLANADE SANDSTONE: The Great Esplanade was the name given by Clarence E. Dutton to the grand avenues of the plateau at Toroweap. He wrote, "...we find its surface to be mostly bare rock, with broad shallow basins etched in them, which hold water after the showers. There are thousands of

146

these pools, and when the showers have passed they gleam and glitter in the sun like innumerable mirrors." D. White formally described the sandstone in 1929, and Edwin McKee named it in 1975. An esplanade is an open, level space used for public walks or drives, or an open space between a fortress and a town. The word is derived from two Latin words: ex- meaning out and planus meaning level. This formation shows a mixed environment and is Permian in age. (36, 130)

RM 15.0

WESCOGAME FORMATION: The Wescogame Formation was named by Edwin McKee in 1975. The type locality is along the Apache Trail which begins in Supai Village and winds up on the east side of Havasu Canyon toward Manakacha Point. Wescogame is a Havasupai family name. Both large-scale cross bedding and evidence of streams and shallow rivers which wandered over a coastal plane indicate both marine and fresh water deposition. (45)

RM 18.0

MANAKACHA FORMATION: The Manakacha Formation was named by Edwin McKee in 1975. The type locality is along the Apache Trail which begins in Supai Village and winds up on the east side of Havasu Canyon toward Manakacha Point. Manakacha is a Havasupai family name meaning who cares for many children. Chief Jasper Manukacha was head chief after Navajo from 1900-1942. The marine deposit shows large-scale cross-bedding which indicates a deep and rough sea environment. (74)

RM 20.2

WATAHOMIGI FORMATION: The Watahomigi Formation was named by Edwin McKee in 1975. The type locality is on the west side of Havasu, northwest of Supai Village, and directly below Watahomigi Point. This Havasupai family name, meaning stripped house, identifies the oldest and entirely marine formation of the Supai Group. Small-scale ripple marks and climbing ripples show the environment to have been a calm and shallow sea. (45)

SURPRISE CANYON FORMATION: The Surprise Canyon Formation was discovered in 1976 by George Billingsley while mapping the geology of western Grand Canyon. He named it after Surprise Canyon and the formation was described by Billingsley and Stanley Beus in 1985. The type locality is ten miles west of Surprise Canyon near the Bat Tower lookout due to the better exposures and accessibility. Differences in rocks at the top of the Redwall Limestone were first noted by other USGS geologists in 1962 and 1969, as well as the NPS in 1964 while doing archeological work around Bright Angel and Transept Canyons. Channels of the Surprise Canyon Formation show it to be a carbonate-clastic estuarine deposit of Mississippian age. (46)

REDWALL LIMESTONE: Powell was first to describe this Mississippian sequence of rocks. In his account he wrote, "Over the alcove sandstone there are 1,600 feet of limestone, in many places a beautiful marble, as in Marble Canyon. As it appears along the Grand Canyon it is always stained a brilliant red, for immediately over it there are thin seams of iron, and the storms have painted these limestones with pigments from above. Altogether this is the redwall group. It is chiefly limestone. Let it be called the red wall limestone." In 1875, G.K. Gilbert formally named the Redwall Limestone after the type locality in Redwall Canyon (a tributary to White Creek in Shinumo Canyon) calling it a group. Its members, described by Edwin McKee in 1963, in descending order are: (83)

> **HORSESHOE MESA MEMBER:** The type locality is Horseshoe Mesa below Grandview Point.
>
> **MOONEY FALLS MEMBER:** The type locality is Mooney Falls in Havasu Canyon.
>
> **THUNDER SPRINGS MEMBER:** The type locality are the cliffs west of Thunder Springs at the head of Thunder River in Tapeats Canyon.
>
> **WHITMORE WASH MEMBER:** The type locality is the Hurricane Fault, about one quarter mile north of the Colorado River on the east side of Whitmore Wash Valley.

TEMPLE BUTTE LIMESTONE OR FORMATION: This Devonian layer was named by Charles Walcott in 1889 for exposures in the vicinity of Temple Butte, located three miles south from the junction of the Colorado with the Little Colorado River on river right. Stanley Beus subsequently called it the Temple Butte Formation in 1973.

UNDIVIDED OR UNCLASSIFIED DOLOMITES: A dolomite is a calcium magnesium carbonate mineral. It resembles limestone and grades into it by changes in the amount of calcite. It is thought to form during slow deposition and by the action of magnesium ions in sea water on calcareous ooze. However, some limestone can be changed to dolomite long after it is deposited and consolidated. The dolomites are undivided or unclassified as no one has yet to formally describe, map, and name this complex rock unit. Geologic immortality awaits the geologist who can tackle the conundrum.

TONTO GROUP: In 1914, Levi Noble proposed the threefold division of the Tonto group and used the names Tapeats Sandstone, Bright Angel Shale, and Muav Limestone to designate the formations. However, these names were also used by Charles Walcott in his 1901 field notes. The group is Cambrian in age. Cambria is the Roman name for Wales, where the first evidence of complex life forms were discovered. Tonto is from the Tonto Plateau, named for the Apaches who were one of the Tonto Basin Indians. Tonto is the Spanish word for fool, a name used erroneously for their supposed foolishness. (45)

MUAV LIMESTONE: The type locality for these gray to rusty orange dolomite and limestone rocks is Muav Canyon in the Shinumo Canyon drainage. Seven members are recognized: Havasu, Gateway Canyon, Kanab Canyon, Peach Springs, Spencer Canyon, Sanup Plateau, and Rampart Cave Members. Muav is a Paiute word meaning divide or pass. (45)

BRIGHT ANGEL SHALE: The type locality for the green and red-brown shale and siltstones of the Bright Angel Shale is Bright Angel Canyon. Eight members are recognized: three are named (Flour Sack, Meriwitica-Tincanebits (sic), and Red-Brown Members), and five are unnamed. Major Powell bestowed the name Bright Angel to contrast the naming of the Dirty Devil (Fremont River) upstream during his 1869 voyage. (83)

RM 58.2

TAPEATS SANDSTONE: The type locality for the Tapeats' tan or reddish-brown sandstone and conglomerate rocks is Tapeats Creek, below which the Colorado River bed lies within the sandstone ledges. Tapeats is named after Ta Pits, the Paiute Indian who told Major Powell that he owned the drainage. (33)

RM 68.5

GREAT UNCOMFORMITY: The term Great Unconformity was first used by John Wesley Powell in 1876. An unconformity is a lack of continuity in deposition between rock strata in contact which corresponds to a period of nondeposition, weathering, or erosion. The Great Unconformity represents a 230 million year break (between 800 and 570 million years ago). It is the erosional surface between the horizontal Paleozoic rocks (Tapeats Sandstone) and the underlying, deformed Precambrian rocks (Grand Canyon Supergroup).

THE PRECAMBRIAN ROCK DIVISIONS:

GRAND CANYON SERIES OR SUPERGROUP: The Grand Canyon Series or Supergroup was named by Major Powell in 1876. In 1914, Levi Noble, who mapped the Shinumo Quadrangle with Francois Matthes in 1908, named the following rock units in the Grand Canyon Series in descending order: Dox Formation, Shinumo Quartzite, Hakatai Shale, Bass Limestone, and Hotauta Conglomerate. The Series was renamed the Grand Canyon Supergroup by Don Elston and G.R. Scott in 1976.

SIXTYMILE FORMATION: T.D. Ford and W.J. Breed named this formation in 1973. The type locality is on the north side of Sixtymile and Awatubi Canyons and the top of Nankoweap Butte. Three members are recognized, the Upper, Middle, and Lower Members.

CHUAR GROUP: The group was named in 1883 by Charles Doolittle Walcott. He divided the Grand Canyon Series into two unconformable groups, the upper Chuar Group and the lower Grand Canyon Group. In 1894, Walcott renamed the Grand Canyon Group, the Unkar Group. Chuar is the shortened form of Chuarrumpeak, a Kaibab chief. The Chuar group is the youn-

150

gest of the Younger Precambrian sequence of rocks and the type locality is Chuar Creek. (45)

KWAGUNT FORMATION: Charles Keyes named this formation or series in 1938. T.D. Ford and W.J. Breed named the members in 1973. Kwagunt was a Paiute Indian who told John Wesley Powell that his father owned Kwagunt Valley and had given it to him. (45)

WALCOTT MEMBER: The type locality is the head of Walcott Glen and the upper northern part of Nankoweap Butte. Charles Doolittle Walcott studied the Grand Canyon Series of rock in 1882-1883. He is called North America's pioneer in the study of Precambrian life. (105)

AWATUBI MEMBER: The type locality is in Awatubi Canyon. Awatubi is an anglicization of a Hopi word meaning high place of the bow people and the location of a pueblo village which was destroyed in 1700. (45)

CARBON BUTTE MEMBER: The type locality Carbon Butte, a prominent remnantal butte on the east side of Chuar Valley. Carbon Butte was named by Charles Walcott. (45)

GALEROS FORMATION: T.D. Ford and W.H. Breed named this formation and most of the associated members in 1973. The type locality is the Galeros Butte, a promontory in Chuar and Carbon Canyons. Galeros is named for Juan Galeras, who was one of the three men sent by Cardenas to climb down to the Colorado River when the party first sighted it from the South Rim in 1540. (54)

DUPPA MEMBER: The type locality is below Duppa Butte in Kwagunt Canyon. Bryan Philip Duppa (1832-1892) was an early resident of the Salt River Valley and proposed the names for Phoenix and Tempe, Arizona. (45)

CARBON CANYON MEMBER: The type locality is the West Fork of Carbon Canyon and middle part of Chuar Canyon. Carbon Canyon was named by the 1923 USGS Birdseye expedition. (10)

JUPITER MEMBER: Charles Keyes named these shales in 1938. The type locality is under Jupiter's Temple.

TANNER MEMBER: Charles Keyes named this in 1922 for outcrops at Tanner's Crossing of the Little Colorado River, at Cameron, Arizona.

RM 68.5

NANKOWEAP FORMATION: Almon H. Thompson called Nankoweap valley Red Shales Valley in 1872. C.E. Van Gundy first described the group in 1934. Later, it was called t'ie Nankoweap Formation by Maxson. The type locality is in Basalt Canyon and on the north side of Nankoweap Valley. There are two members recognized, the Upper and Lower. Nankoweap is the Paiute word for place where Indians had a fight or the word meaning singing or echoing. (33, 45, 58, 110)

UNKAR GROUP: Charles Doolittle Walcott first described the group in detail in 1894 for outcrops in Unkar Valley. The upper part was reassigned to the Nankoweap Group. Levi Noble subdivided the five formations listed below in 1914. Unkar means red creek or red stone in Paiute. (42, 54)

RM 65.5

CARDENAS BASALT: Named the Cardenas Lavas by Charles Keyes in 1938, the Cardenas Basalt was formally redesignated by Don Elston in 1988. Lava is a hot fluid, so the term basalt is given to the solidified rock. The type locality is Cardenas Butte at the base of which the full sequence is exposed. Garcia Lopez de Cardenas and his men were the first foreigners to see the Grand Canyon from the South Rim in 1540. In 1961, Maxson proposed the name Rama Formation for the basalt flows, diabase dikes and sills, though the name was not accepted by the USGS Geologic Names Committee. (45)

DOX FORMATION: First called the Dox Sandstone by Levi Noble in 1914, it was redesigned by G.M. Stevenson in 1973 and G.M. Stevenson and Stanely Beus in 1982. The type locality is Dox Castle underneath which a typical section is found below the Tonto Group. Four members are recognized: the Upper, Upper Middle, Lower Middle, and Lower, however these informal position names are sometimes called the Ochoa Point, Comanche Point, Solomon Temple, and Escalante Creek Members. Miss Virginia Dox, from Cincinnati, Ohio was the first female visitor guided by William W. Bass in western Grand Canyon. It is said that she was voluptuous and had beautiful red hair. (55)

RM 74.8

SHINUMO QUARTZITE: The type locality is Shinumo Creek. Four members are recognized, the Upper, Upper Middle, Lower Middle, and Lower. Shinumo is the Paiute word meaning old people or cliff dwellers, in reference to the Anasazis, a Navajo word for the early Basketmaker and Pueblo Indians. (45)

RM 76.2

HAKATAI SHALE: The type locality is Hakatai Canyon where it is well exposed. Three members are recognized, the Upper, Middle, and Lower. Hakatai is the Havasupai word applied to the Grand Canyon meaning a large, roaring sound caused by a fierce wind or the dashing of the waters. (45, 54)

RM 77.0

BASS LIMESTONE: The type locality is Bass Canyon. William Wallace Bass (1841-1933) was a miner and guide in western Grand Canyon. (45)

RM 77.5

HOTAUTA CONGLOMERATE MEMBER: The type locality is Hotauta Canyon. Hotauta was the son of Chief Navajo, the last great Havasupai Indian chief. (44, 45, 55, 56)

GREATEST ANGULAR UNCONFORMITY: Levi Noble named the contact between the base of the Grand Canyon Supergroup and the Vishnu Group the Greatest Angular Unconformity in 1914. This break represents 425 million years of erosion from 1,675 to 1,250 million years ago. The Greatest Angular Unconformity merges with the Great Unconformity a short distance downstream of Hance Rapids about 1,000 ft above the river. The two unconformities meet where the base of the Tapeats Sandstone adjoins the Vishnu Group, a truly great unconformity representing 1,200 million years. During this time, nearly 12,000 ft of rock were removed by erosion.

The Early Proterozoic or Older Precambrian rocks can be divided into three subdivisions. The Vishnu Metamorphic Complex is the best known, while the felsic gneisses (Trinity Gneiss and Elves Chasm Gneiss) and Zoroaster Plutonic Complex (weakly foliated to directionless plutons and pegmatite/aplite dikes and sills) complete the complex picture.

VISHNU METAMORPHIC COMPLEX OR VISHNU SCHIST: The Vishnu Schist was first named the Vishnu terrane by Clarence D. Walcott in 1890. Redesignated the Vishnu Schist by Noble in 1914, it was studied by Noble and Hunter in 1916. Geologists now call the complex unit the Vishnu Metamorphic Complex. The metamorphosed sedimentary and minor volcanic materials were deposited in a marine environment about two billion years ago. Schist is a fine-grained metamorphic rock. The type locality for the Vishnu Schist is at the Colorado River at Vishnu Creek. Vishnu was the redeemer or preserver in the Hindu religion. (45)

In 1938, Cambell and Maxson subdivided the Vishnu Schist into an older, metamorphosed, sedimentary unit (Vishnu Series) and a younger, metamorphosed, volcanic unit (Brahma Series). Later, Maxson submitted the name Brahma Schist for the vertically standing bands in in the Vishnu Schist. Presently, the name Brahma Schist is not considered valid, but the subject is debated by geologists. Maxson's Brahma Schist type locality is the Inner Gorge of Grand Canyon. (10)

TRINITY GNEISS AND ELVES CHASM GNEISS: R.S. Babcock and other workers from 1972 to 1979 named these gneisses, which are enigmatic to geologists. The name is derived after the type localities of Trinitiy Creek and Elves Chasm. Gneiss is defined as a coarse-grained metamorphic rock with bands or layers of visably unlike composition; for example, feldspar-rich layers alternateing with mica-rich layers.

ZOROASTER PLUTONIC COMPLEX: This complex is comprised of weakly foliated to directionless plutons (seen at RM 90.8, 96.2, and 97.7) and pegmatite and aplite dikes and sills (seen at RM 80.5). About twenty small bodies of plutons are scattered throughout the canyon. Some are well exposed at Pipe Creek, Phantom Canyon, and Tuna Creek. Plutons are rocks that are of intrusive, igneous origin which solidify or crystallize deep within the earth's mantle and are revealed when exposed by erosion or penetrated by wells or mines. Pegmatites are characterized by large grain size, while aplites are fine- to medium-grained. Dikes cut across the bedding layers of other rocks, while sills spread between bedding layers.

The dikes and sills were first studied by Campbell in 1937. In 1938, Campbell and Maxson named these rocks the Zoroaster Granite after the type locality in Zoroaster Creek. The white, pink, or red granitic igneous rocks have feldspar as the chief mineral, as well as quartz. They are thought to have originated by hydrothermal solutions and replacement in fissures or open spaces. Zoroaster was the Persian founder of the Zoroastrian religion, in the region now known as Iran. (45)

ANASAZI: Anasazi is a Navajo word meaning the ancient ones, though the modern translation is enemy ancestors or ancient enemies. The Anasazi Indians are separated into the Basketmakers and the Pueblo Anasazi. The Basketmakers (100 B.C. to 450 A.D.) hunted with spears, atlatls, bows, and arrows. They are so named because of their distinctive baskets. They showed the beginnings of agriculture, community living, horticulture, and were hunter/gatherers. The Pueblo Anasazi (750 to 1150 A.D.) decorated and fired ceramic pottery, built pueblo dwellings, and worshiped in kivas. The Grand Canyon was abandoned by the Pueblo Anasazi for unknown reasons, though drought may have been the cause, about 1200. The Hopi Indians, their descendants, called them Hisatwuwuyom or Hisatsinom meaning ancient ones or ancestors. (45, 54, 91)

COHONINA: The Cohonina Indians occupied the area between central Arizona and the South Rim from 700-1150 A.D. They were hunter-gatherers and made two types of pottery. One style imitated the ceramic styles of other cultures by using a red wash on their gray pottery, while the other style was distinctive of their culture. The Cohonina disappeared around 1150. (45)

HAVASUPAI: The Havasupai Indians originally were part of the Hualapai who settled in Havasu and Cataract Canyons. During the late 1700s to early 1800s the Havasupai were seen by anthropologists as a separate group. Havasupai means people who live where it is green or people of the blue-green water. The reservation was created in 1880 and the center is the village of Supai. They were sometimes called the Coconinos, the Cosninos, the Cosninas, Kohonino, Kuhnikwe, and Yampais. (45, 95, 107)

HOPI: The Hopi Indians are descendants of the Pueblo peoples and the Sinagua Indians. The Hopi are dry-land farmers and have many ceremonies and traditions. One village, Old Oraibi, was founded in 1150 and has been continuously inhabited to today. Antonio Espejo, a Spanish explorer, visited northern Arizona in 1582-83. He called the Hopi villages, Mohoce and mentioned five pueblos. Mohoce or Mochis was the name given the Hopi by the eastern Pueblos, meaning awl people for their bone needles. This term may have been distorted to Moqui or Moki. Moki means green, blue, or blue-green; desirous of or in need of; a sack full, or deer. A similar word mokee is detestable to the Hopi as a name for their people since in their language it means dead. The term Hopi was adopted from Hopitu by the Smithsonian Institution in 1895. Hopitu is the name used by the tribe for itself, meaning the Peaceful Ones. The Hopi Indian Reservation was established in 1882 with the tribal headquarters at Kykotsmovi, on Second Mesa. The Hopi Reservation is wholly surrounded by the Navajo Indian Reservation. (45, 54, 91)

HUALAPAI: The Hualapai Indians were originally a tribe of Yuman Cerbat Indians living from the middle portion of the Colorado River to the interior of Arizona in the Hualapai, Sacramento, and Yavapai Valleys and in the Cerbat and Aquarius Mountains. A reservation was established in 1883 and the headquarters is at Peach Springs. The word Hualapai or Walapai means people of the tall pines. (45, 54)

NAVAJO: From 1000-1400 A.D., the Apaches and Navajo Indians, both Athabascan peoples, migrated to the Southwest from Canada. Pueblo people first called the Navajo the Apaches de Navahu, meaning our enemies with cultivated fields. The word apachu means enemy and/or strangers, nave means field, and the word ajo is a Spanish suffix meaning small. By the 1800s, the Navajo settled and raised crops in northern Arizona, while the Apaches traveled to southern Arizona and Mexico and remained exclusively hunters and raiders. The Navajo Indian Reservation was established in 1895 and the tribal headquarters are in Window Rock. (39, 45, 54)

PAIUTE: The Paiute Indians are a Shoshonean people who came from the Great Basin deserts of Nevada and western Utah. Paiute possibly means true people in the Shoshonean dialect. Many tribes were recognized, but in the Grand Canyon region, Powell was first to document the lives of the Kaibab, Shivwitz, and Uinkaret clans. In 1934, Isabel Kelly, an ethnographer, declared the Southern Paiute extinct. The Kaibab Indian Reservation was created in 1907 and the center is Pipe Springs, on the Arizona Strip. (45, 54, 58)

APPENDIX A: SUMMARY OF PLACE NAMES BY AUTHOR

Below is a chronological and alphabetical list of place names bestowed by the main explorers, scientists, historians, government workers, and river runners in Grand Canyon for locations mentioned in the body of this book. The list is not complete, as it is not always known who bestowed the names. Words derived from Indian words are also listed by tribe. Names in parentheses list either specific persons or the place name which is in common usage. A question mark means there is some uncertainty or question as to who actually named the place.

John Wesley Powell and his Companions: Barbenceta Butte, Beaver Creek (A.H. Thompson), Bright Angel Creek, Catastrophe Rapid (A.H. Thompson, = Separation Rapids), Chocolate Cliffs, De Motte Park, Echo Peaks (F.S. Dellenbaugh), Escalante Creek, Glen Canyon, Grand Canyon, Grapevine Creek (?), Great Unconformity, House Rock Valley (F.M. Dellenbaugh), Kanab Plateau, Kwagunt Canyon, Mollie's Nipple (Thompson), Mount Dellenbaugh, Mount Emma, Mount Logan, Mount Trumbull, Nankoweap Canyon, Redwall Limestone, Rio Colorado Chiquito (= Little Colorado River), Sapphire Canyon, Shinumo Altar (F.M. Dellenbaugh), Shinumo Creek, Sockdolager Rapids, Stewart's Canyon (= Jumpup), Surprise Valley (E.O. Beaman), Tapeats Creek, Turquoise Canyon, Uinkaret Mountains and Plateau, Vasey's Paradise, and Vermillion Cliffs.

Robert Brewster Stanton: The Cathedral (now unnamed), Bridle or Bridal Falls (= Deer Creek Falls), McDonald Creek (= Crystal Creek), Point Hansbrough, Point Retreat (no unnamed), and Southern Gateway (= Grand Wash Cliffs).

Charles Doolittle Walcott: Carbon Butte, Congress Canyon (= Hance Canyon), and Vishnu Schist.

Clarence Edward Dutton and Henry Gannet (HG): Brahma Temple, Buddha Temple (HG), Cape Final, Cape Royal, Deva Temple (CD and HG), Hindu Amphitheater, Horn Creek (HG), Milk Creek, Mount Emma, Palisades, Parissawampitts Spring, Point Sublime, Powell Plateau, Salt Creek (HG), Shiva Temple, The Transept, Vishnu Creek and Temple, Vulcan's Throne, Zoroaster Canyon and Temple.

Francois Emile Matthes: Ariel Point, Apollo Temple, Awatubi Canyon, Brahma Temple, De Vaca Terrace, Evolution Amphitheater,

Explorers Canyon (= Conquistador Aisle), The Inferno, Krishna Shrine, Lipan Point, Ribbon Fall, Solomon Temple, Tilted Mesa, Walhalla Plateau and Glades, and Wotan's Throne.

William Wallace Bass: Copper Canyon, Garnet Canyon, Grand Scenic Divide, Serpentine Canyon, and White Creek.

George Wharton James: Aisle of Cardenas (=Stephens Aisle, Alarcon Aisle (=Conquistador Aisle), Angels Gate, Apache Point (?), Beaver Falls (?), Cheops Pyramid (?), Dana Butte, Dox Castle (?), Dutton Point and Canyon, Hotauta Canyon (?), Observation Plateau (= Huxley Terrace), Marsh Butte, Temple of Om (= Tyndall Dome), Thurso Butte (= Wallace Butte, Yaki Point, and Yucatan Temple (= Scylla Butte).

Emery and Ellsworth Kolb: Battleship Iowa (= Battleship), Breezy Point, Bridge of Sighs, Cape Desolation (= Cape Solitude), Cheyava Falls, Christmas Rapid (= Walthenburg Rapids), Last Portage (= Lava Cliff Rapids), and Surprise Falls (= Deer Creek Falls).

Richard T. Evans and USGS Topographers (*): Agate Canyon, Aztec Amphitheater (?), Bedivere Point, Centeotl Point, Elaine Castle, Excalibur, Forster Canyon, Fossil Canyon, Gawain Abyss, Galahad Point, Guinevere Castle, King Arthur Castle, Lancelot Point, Merlin Abyss, Modred Abyss, Montezuma Point, Mount Wodo, Point Huitzil, Point Quetzal, Rainbow Plateau (*), Reference Point (?), Specter Chasm (*), Toltec Point, and Tulip Point (*, = Swamp Point).

Claude H. Birdseye and the 1923 USGS Survey: Bottleneck Canyon (= Surprise Canyon), Bridge Canyon, Carbon Canyon, Granite Narrows, Granite Park Canyon, Granite Spring Canyon, House Rock Rapids, Indian Canyon, Neighing Horse Canyon (= 140 Mile Canyon), President Harding Rapids, Royal Arches, Sheer Wall Rapids, Spring Cave Rapid (= Cave Springs Rapids), Tanner Rapids, Three Springs Canyon, Triple Alcoves, Triumphal Arch (?), and Upset Rapids.

National Park Service: Fire Point, Johnson Point, Sinking Ship, Slate Creek, Sturdevant Point, Swamp Point, Temple Butte, Uncle Jim Point, and Wall Creek; and probably Demaray Point, Mather Point, and Schellbach Butte.

Frank Bond (Board on Geographic Names): Arrowhead Terrace, Bedrock Canyon, Blacktail Canyon and Valley, Devils Slide Rapids,

Espejo Creek and Butte, Hattan Butte, Jones Point, Kibbey Butte, Mount Hayden, Ochoa Point, and Papago Creek.

Will C. Barnes: Bourke Point, Hubbel Butte, Seiber Point Sullivan Peak, and Tritle Peak.

Pat T. Reilly: Brown's Cove, Brown Inscription, Brown's Riffle, Hansbrough-Richards Rapids, Hislop Cave, Johnson Point, and Keyhole Natural Bridge.

River Runners (only some of the many names!): Christmas Tree Cave, Doll's House, Eye of Odin, Evan's Heaven, Forever Eddy, Four Second Waterfall, Furnace Flats, Helicopter Eddy, Havazoo, Honeymoon Rapid, Hualapai Acres, Last Chance, Ledges, Nixon Rock, Owl Camp and Canyon, Poncho's Kitchen, Rancid Tuna Fish Sandwich Rock, Randy's Rock, Rattlesnake Camp, Ross Wheeler, Six Pack Eddy, and Upset Hotel.

Havasupai Indian words: Akaba, Chickapanagi, Hamidreek, Hakatai, Hotauta, Havasu, Manakacha, Matkatamiba, Moenave (?), Mulgullo, Olo, Uqualla, Panameta, Panya, Paya, Supai, Tithumigi, Topocoba, Watahomigie, Wescogame, Wigleeya, Wodo, Yumtheska, and Yunosi.

Hopi Indian words: Awatubi, Coconino, Honan, Moenkopi, Nachi, Sipapu, Tiyo, and Wala.

Hualapai Indian words: Beecher, Honga, Meriwhitica, and Moko or Mono.

Navajo Indian words: Ah Hol Sah, Chinle, Hot Na Na, Kayenta, Leche-e, Sase Nasket, Tatahatso, and Tatahoysa.

Paiute Indian words: Boysag, Kaibab, Kanab, Kanabownits, Kwagunt, Muav, Nankoweap, Obi, Paguekwash, Parashant, Paria, Parissawampitts, Shanub, Shinarump, Shinumo, Shivwits, Tincanebitts (?), Toroweap, Tuweep, Uinkaret, and Unkar.

APPENDIX B: MILEAGE PLACE NAMES

The following is a list of recognized tributaries and rapids (7, 97) along the Colorado River between Lee's Ferry and Pearce Ferry which are not listed in the body of this book. These washes, canyons, creeks, and rapids only have mileage designation names, referencing their location by river mile below Lee's Ferry. Most of these names were given by the Claude H. Birdseye 1923 Survey, however later river runner have named places by referencing the river mileage. On topographic maps, the number is spelled out.

3 Mile Wash	138 1/2 Mile Rapids
4 Mile Wash	135 Mile Rapids
5 Mile Wash	141 Mile Rapids
6 Mile Wash	144 1/2 Mile Rapids
13 Mile Rapids	164 Mile Rapids
18 Mile Wash	185 Mile Rapids
19 Mile Canyon	187 Mile Rapids
22 Mile Wash	192 Mile Canyon
23 Mile Rapids	194 Mile Canyon
23 1/2 Mile Rapids	193 Mile Canyon
24 Mile Rapids	196 Mile Creek
27 Mile Rapids	205 Mile Creek
29 Mile Rapids	209 Mile Canyon and Rapids
36 Mile Rapids	214 Mile Creek
60 Mile Canyon and Rapids	215 Mile Creek
91 Mile Creek	217 Mile Canyon and Rapids
94 Mile Creek	222 Mile Canyon
104 Mile Rapids	224 Mile Canyon and Rapids
110 Mile Rapids	228 Mile Canyon
119 Mile Creek	231 Mile Rapids
122 Mile Creek	232 Mile Rapids
127 Mile Creek	237 Mile Rapids
128 Mile Creek and Rapids	240 Mile Rapids
133 Mile Creek	241 Mile Rapids

BIBLIOGRAPHY

1. Alter, J. Cecil (editor). 1939. Diary of Almon Harris Thompson. Utah Hist. Quart., Vol. 7, No. 1-3, 204 pg.
2. Austin, Mary. 1924. Land of Journey's Ending. Century Pub. Co., New York, 459 pg.
3. Baker, Pearl. 1970. Trail on the Water. Pruett Pub. Co., Boulder, 134 pg + maps.
4. Barnes, Will C. 1988. Arizona Place Names. The University of Arizona Press, Tucson, 503 pg.
5. Bartlett, Richard A. 1962. Great Surveys of the American West. Univ. of Oklahoma Press, Norman, 408 pg.
6. Beatty, William. 1962. Geology and Mining Operations in the United States. Guano Cave, Mohave Co., Arizona. Cave Notes 4(5):40-41.
7. Belknap, Buzz and Loie B. Evans. 1991. Grand Canyon River Guide. Westwater Books, Evergreen, 96 pg.
8. Bender, Gordon L. (editor). 1982. Reference Handbook on the Deserts of North America. Greenwood Press, Westport, 594 pg.
9. Bertelt, Guillermo. 1980. Navajo Place-Names in Arizona. The Southwest Museum. The Masterkeys, 54(2): 45-52.
10. Birdseye, Claude H. 1923. Diary of the Grand Canyon Survey 1923. Typewritten manuscript, unpublished, 86 pg.
11. Birdseye, C.H. and R.C. Moore. 1924. A Boat Voyage Through the Grand Canyon of the Colorado. Geographical Review, 14(2): 177-196.
12. Boner, F.C. et al. 1990. Water Resources Data for Arizona, Water Year 1989. USGS Water Data Report AZ-89-1, 396 pg.
13. Breed, William J. and Evelyn C. Roat (editors). 1974. Geology of the Grand Canyon, Museum of Northern Arizona and Grand Canyon Natural History Association, 185 pg.
14. Brooks, Juanita. 1973. John Doyle Lee: Zealot, Pioneer Builder, Scapegoat. Arthur C. Clark Co., Glendale, 404 pg.
15. Ibid. 1984. Emma Lee. Utah State Univ. Press, Logan, 112 pg.
16. Butchart, Harvey. 1965. The Lower Gorge of the Little Colorado. Arizona Highways 14:34-42.
17. Ibid. 1985. Grand Canyon Treks III. La Siesta Press, Glendale, 72 pg.
18. Ibid. 1989. Grand Canyon Treks II. La Siesta Press, Glendale, 48 pg.
19. Ibid. 1990. Grand Canyon Treks. La Siesta Press, Glendale, 71 pg.
20. Carrell, Toni (editor), J.E. Bradford, and W. L Rusho. 1987. Charles H. Spencer's Mining Operation and Paddle Wheel Steamboat. Submerged Cultural Resources Site Report. Glen Canyon National Recreation Area. Southwest Cultural Resources Center Professional Papers No. 13., Santa Fe, 165 + maps.
21. Chalfant, James M. (editor). 1982. Colorado River Controversies, by Robert Brewster Stanton. Reprint edition, Westwater Books, Boulder City, 261 pg.
22. Cobb, Irvin S. 1913. Roughing It De Luxe. George Doran Co., New York, 219 pg.
23. Cook, William. 1987. The WEN, the Botany, and the Mexican Hat. The Adventures of the First Women Through the Grand Canyon on the Nevills Expedition. Callisto Books, Orangeville, 151 pg.
24. Cooley, John. 1988. The Great Unknown. The Journals of the Historic First Expedition Down the Colorado River. Northland Publishing, Flagstaff, 207 pg.

25. Cooley, M.E. 1976. Spring Flow From Pre-Pennsylvanian Rocks in the Southwestern Part of the Navajo Indian Reservation, Arizona. Geological Survey Professional Paper 521-F, U.S. Gov't Printing Office, Washington, 15 pg. + maps.

26. Ibid., B.N. Aldridge, and R.C. Euler. 1977. Effects of the Catastrophic Flood of December 1966, North Rim Area, Eastern Grand Canyon, Arizona. USGS Prof. Paper 980, U.S. Government Printing Office, Washington, 43 pg + maps.

27. Cox, Nellie Iverson. 1973. Footprints on the Arizona Strip (with accent on "Bundyville"). Horizon Publishers, Bountiful, 256 pg.

28. Ibid. A Harsh Land and Proud. 1982. Saga of the "Arizona Strip." Cox Printing Co., Las Vegas, 350 pg + appendices.

29. Crampton, C. Gregory and D.L. Smith (editors). 1961. The Hoskaninni Papers. Mining in Glen Canyon, 1897-1902 by Robert B. Stanton. Anthro. Papers No. 54 (Glen Canyon Series No. 15). Univ. of Utah, Salt Lake City, 177 pg.

30. Crampton, C. Gregory. 1972. Land of Living Rock. The Grand Canyon and the High Plateaus: Arizona, Utah, Nevada. Alfred A. Knopf, New York, 275 pg.

31. Crumbo, Kim. 1981. A River Runner's Guide to the History of the Grand Canyon. Johnson Books, Boulder, 61 pg + maps.

32. Dellenbaugh, Frederick S. 1962. The Romance of the Colorado River. First published in 1904. The Johnson Pub. Co., Boulder, 399 pg.

33. Ibid. 1962. A Canyon Voyage. A narrative of the Second Powell Expedition down the Green-Colorado River from Wyoming, and the Explorations on Land, in the Years 1871 and 1872. First Published in 1908. The Univ. of Arizona Press, Tucson, 277 pg.

34. Dobyns, H.F. and R.C. Euler. 1976. The Walapai People. Indian Tribal Series, Phoenix.

35. Dubendorff, Seymour S. 1909. Notes Taken While on the Green and Colorado River. Unpublished, typewritten manuscript, 10 pg.

36. Dutton, Clarence. 1977. The Tertiary History of the Grand Canyon District, with Atlas. USGS Mon. 2, Published in 1882, Peregrine Smith, Inc., Layton, 264 pg.

37. Eddy, Clyde. 1929. Down the World's Most Dangerous River. Frederick A. Stokes, Co., New York. 293 pg.

38. Eiseman, F.B., Jr. 1959. The Hopi Salt Trail. Plateau 32(2):25-32.

39. Elwood, Lloyd. 1933. Arizonology. Coconino Sun, Flagstaff, AZ. 92 pg.

40. Euler, Robert C. (editor). 1984. The Archaeology, Geology, and Paleobiology of Stanton's Cave, Grand Canyon National Park. Grand Canyon Nat. Hist. Assoc., Mono. No. 6, 139 pg + appendices.

41. Flavell, George F. 1987. The Log of the Panthon. An Account of an 1896 River Voyage from Green River, Wyoming to Yuma, Arizona through the Grand Canyon. Edited by Neil B. Carmony and David E. Brown. Pruett Pub., Boulder, 109 pg.

42. Fowler, Don D. 1972. Photographed All the Best Scenery. Jack Hiller's Diary of the Powell Expeditions 1871-1875. Univ. of Utah Press, Salt Lake, 225 pg.

43. Ibid., Robert C. Euler, and Catherine S. Fowler. 1969. John Wesley Powell and the Anthropology of the Canyon Country. Geological Survey Professional Paper 670, U.S. Government Printing Office, Washington, 30 pg.

44. Granger, Byrd Howell. 1983. Arizona's Names (X Marks the Place). The Falconer Pub. Co, Tucson, 824 pg.

45. Ibid. 1960. Will C. Barnes' Arizona Place Names. Revised and enlarged. Univ. of Arizona Press, Tucson, 519 pg. Also, Grand Canyon Place Names. 1960. A separate chapter of the above book, printed as a 26 pg. booklet.

163

46. Grover, P.W. 1989. Stratigraphy and Depositional Environment of the Surprise Canyon Formation. Ph.D. dissertation, Northern Arizona University, Flagstaff.
47. Hall, Sharlot M. 1975. Sharlot Hall on the Arizona Strip. Edited by C. Gregory Crampton, Northland Press, Flagstaff, 97 pg.
48. Hamblin W. Kenneth and J. Keith Rigby. 1968. Guidebook to the Colorado River, Part 1: Lee's Ferry to Phantom Ranch in Grand Canyon National Park. Vol. 15, Part 5, Studies for Students No. 4. Brigham Young University, Provo, 84 pg.
49. Ibid. 1969. Guidebook to the Colorado River, Part 2: Phantom Ranch in Grand Canyon National Park to Lake Mead, Arizona-Nevada. Vol. 16, Part 2, Studies for Students No. 5. Brigham Young University, Provo, 126 pg.
50. Hamblin, W.K. and J.R. Murphy. 1969. Grand Canyon Perspectives. A Guide to the Canyon Scenery by Means of Interpretive Panoramas. Brigham Young University Geology Studies, Special Publication No. 1, Provo, 48 pg.
51. Hamilton, Edith. 1953. Mythology. Little, Brown & Co., New York, 335 pg.
52. Hoffmeister, Donald F. 1971. Mammals of Grand Canyon. Univ. of Illinois Press, Urbana, 183 pg.
53. Horn, Tom. 1964. Life of Tom Horn: Government Scout and Interpreter. Univ. of Oklahoma Press, Norman, 277 pg.
54. Hughes, J. Donald. 1978. In the House of Stone and Light. A Human History of the Grand Canyon. Grand Canyon Natural History Assn., 137 pp.
55. James, George Wharton. 1942. In and Around the Grand Canyon. The Grand Canyon of the Colorado River in Arizona. Little, Brown, and Co. Boston, 352 pg.
56. Ibid. 1910. The Grand Canyon of Arizona. How to See It. Little, Brown, and Co., Kansas City, 265 pg.
57. Johnston, Philip. 1939. Peshlakai Atsidi (1850?-1939). Plateau 12(2):21-25.
58. Kelly, Isabel T. 1964. Southern Paiute Ethnography. Anthro. Papers, No. 69. Univ. of Utah. (Glen Canyon Series No. 21). Johnson Reprint Corp. 1971, 194 pg.
59. Keroher, Grace C. 1970. Lexicon of geologic names of the United States for 1961-1967. USGS Bull. 1350, 4341 pg.
60. Kolb, Ellsworth L. 1952. Through the Grand Canyon from Wyoming to Mexico. MacMillian Co., New York, 344 pg.
61. Krutch, Joseph W. 1958. Grand Canyon, Today and All Its Yesterdays. William Sloane Assoc., New York, 276 pg.
62. Lavender, David. 1982. Colorado River Country. E.P. Dutton, Inc., New York, 238 pg.
63. Ibid. River Runners of the Grand Canyon. 1985. Grand Canyon Natural History Assn. and Univ. of Arizona Press, Tucson, 147 pg.
64. Lockwood, Frank C. 1943. More Arizona Characters. Univ. of Ariz. General Bull. No. 6, Vol. 13(3):1-79.
65. Lowe, Sam. 1988. The Little Colorado River. Arizona Highways, 64(6): 22-31.
66. Luttrell, Gwendolyn W. et al. 1981. Lexicon of geologic names of the United States for 1968-1975. USGS Bull, 1520, 342 pg.
67. Malach, Roman. 1975. Peach Springs in Mohave County. Graphicopy, New York, 48 pg.
68. Marston, Otis. 1960. River Runners: Fast Water Navigation. Utah Hist. Quart. 37(3): 291-308.
69. Martin, P.S., B.E. Sabels, and D. Sutler Jr. 1961. Rampart Cave Coprolite and Ecology of Shasta Ground Sloth. Amer. Journ. of Science, Vol. 259, pg. 102-107.
70. Matthes, Francois E. and Richard T. Evans. 1926. Map of Grand Canyon National Park. The Military Engineer, 18(99): 188-201.

71. Matthes, Francois E. 1967. The Grand Canyon of the Colorado River. On reverse of Bright Angel Quadrangle, 15 minute Series, USGS, one sheet.
72. Maurer, Stephen G. 1983. Solitude and Sunshine. Images of a Grand Canyon Childhood. Pruett Pub. Co., Boulder, 97 pg.
73. Maxson, John H. 1968. Geologic History of the Bright Angel Quadrangle. On reverse, Geologic Map of the Bright Angel Quadrangle, Grand Canyon National, Park, Arizona. Grand Canyon Natural History Assn., one sheet.
74. McKee, Barbara and Edwin, and Joyce Herold. 1975. Havasupai Baskets and Their Makers: 1930-1940. Northland Press, Flagstaff, 142 pg.
75. Measeles, Evelyn Brack. 1981. Lee's Ferry, A Crossing on the Colorado. Pruett Pub. Co., Boulder, 130 pg.
76. Nevills, Norman. Date unknown. Typewritten biography manuscript on file at U.S. Board on Geographic Names, Reston, 6 pg.
77. Noble, Levi F. 1914. The Shinumo Quadrangle, Grand Canyon District, Arizona. USGS Bull. 549, 100 pg + map.
78. Ibid. 1922. A Section of the Paleozoic Formations of the Grand Canyon at the Bass Trail. USGS Prof. Paper 131-B, 73 pg.
79. Orth, Donald J. 1988. Principles, Policies and Procedures: Domestic Geographic Names. United States Board on Geographic Names. U.S. Govt. Printing Office, Washington, 43 pg.
80. Palmer, Wm. A. 1928. Indian Names in Utah Geography. Utah Hist. Quart., I, 5-26.
81. Peattie, Roderick (editor). 1948. The Inverted Mountains: Canyons of the West. The Vanguard Press, Inc., New York, 219 pg.
82. Pewe, Troy L. 1969. Colorado River Guidebook. A Geologic and Geographic Guide from Lee's Ferry to Phantom Ranch. Troy L. Pewe, Tempe, 78 pg.
83. Powell, John, W. 1961. The Exploration of the Colorado River and Its Canyons. First published in 1895. Dover Publication, Inc., New York, 400 pg.
84. Pyne, Stephen J. 1989. Fire on the Rim. A Firefighter's Season at the Grand Canyon. Weidenfeld and Nicolson, New York, 323 pg.
85. Rider, Rowland W. 1979. Sixshooters and Sagebrush. Cowboy Stories of the Southwest. Edited by Deirdre Paulsen. Brigham Young Univ. Press, 152 pg. Reprinted 1985 as The Roll Away Saloon. Utah State Univ. Press, Salt Lake City, 114 pg.
86. Roeske, R.H. 1991. Flood of September 3, 1990 in Havasu Creek Above Mouth Near Supai, AZ, unpublished, provisional USGS report, 4 pg.
87. Rusho, W.L. and C.G. Crampton. 1981. Desert River Crossing. Historic Lee's Ferry on the Colorado River. Peregrine Smith, Salt Lake City, 126 pg. Revised and expanded edition published 1992, 180 pg.
88. Sapir, Edward. 1930. Southern Paiute, a Shoshonean Language. Proc. of the Amer. Acad. of Arts & Sciences, 65(13):1-730.
89. Sargent, R.H. 1942. Colonel Claude Hale Birdseye. Annals of the Assoc. of American Geographers, 32(3):309-315.
90. Scharff, Robert (editor) 1967. Grand Canyon National Park. David McKay Co., Inc., New York, 198 pg.
91. Seaman, P. David. 1985. Hopi Dictionary. Northern Arizona University Anthro. Paper No. 2, Flagstaff, 603 pg.
92a. Simmons, George C. and David L. Gaskill. 1979. River Runners' Guide to the Canyons of the Green and Colorado Rivers With Emphasis on Geologic Features. Volume III: Marble Gorge and Grand Canyon. Northland Press, Flagstaff, 132 pg.

92b. Simmons, George C. and Virginia M. Simmons. 1977. First Photographers of the Grand Canyon. The American West, 14(4):34-38, 61-63.

93. Simpson, George G. 1934. Attending Marvels, a Patagonian Journal. The MacMillian Co., New York, 295 pg.

94. Smith, Dwight L. and C.G. Crampton (editors). 1987. The Colorado River Survey. Robert B. Stanton and the Denver, Colorado Canyon & Pacific Railroad. Howe Brothers, Salt Lake City, 305 pg.

95. Spier, Leslie. 1928. Havasupai Ethnography. Anthro. Papers of the American Museum of Nat. History, New York, 29(3):1-392.

96. Stephens, Hal G. and Eugene M. Shoemaker. 1987. In the Footsteps of John Wesley Powell. An Album of Comparative Photographs of the Green and Colorado River, 1871-72 and 1968. Johnson Books, Boulder, 286 pg.

97. Stevens, Larry. 1983. The Colorado River in Grand Canyon: A Guide. Red Lake Books, Flagstaff, 107 pg.

98. Stone, Julius F. 1932. Canyon Country. The Romance of a Drop of Water and a Grain of Sand. G.P. Putnam's Sons, New York, 442 pg.

99. Talayesva, Don C. 1942. Sun Chief, An Autobiography of a Hopi Indian. Edited by Leo W. Simmons. Yale University Press, New Haven, 460 pg.

100. Thybony, Scott. 1985. Navajo Tribal Parks. A Guide to Hiking Routes. Unpublished, 13 pg.

101. Tillotson, M.R. and Frank J. Taylor. 1949. Grand Canyon Country. Stanford University Press, 108 pg.

102. Trimble, Marshall. 1986. Roadside History of Arizona. Mountain Press Pub. Co., Missoula, 480 pg.

103. Udall, Stewart L. 1987. To the Inland Empire. Doubleday & Co., Garden City, 222 pg.

104. Verkamp, Margaret M. 1940. History of Grand Canyon National Park. Master of Arts Thesis. University of Arizona, Tucson, 88 pg.

105. Walcott, Charles D. 1894. Pre-Cambrian Igneous Rocks of the Unkar Terrace, Grand Canyon of the Colorado, Arizona. USGS 14th Annual Report, Part 2, pg 497-524.

106. Waters, Frank. 1963. Book of the Hopi. Viking Press, New York, 347 pg.

107. Weber, Steven A. and P. David Seaman (editors). 1985. Hava-supai Habitat. A.F. Whiting's Ethnography of a Traditional Indian Culture. Univ. of Ariz. Press, Tucson, 288 pg.

108. Wexler, Mark. 1978. The Naming (and Misnaming) of America. National Wildlife, 16(5):12-16.

109. Wilmarth, Grace M. 1957. Lexicon of Geologic Names of the U.S. (including Alaska). USGS Bull. 896, Vol. 1 & 2.

110. Wilson, Allie Kathleen. 1941. History of the Arizona Strip to 1913. Masters Thesis, Northern Arizona University, Flagstaff, 88 pg.

111. Woods, G. K. (editor). 1899. Personal Impressions of the Grand Canyon of the Colorado near Flagstaff, Arizona as seen through nearly two thousand eyes, and written in the private visitor's book of the world-famous guide Capt. John Hance, guide, story-teller, and path-finder. Whitaker and Ray Co., San Francisco, 163 pg.

Letters: On file at U.S. Board on Geographic Names, Grand Canyon file, Reston, Virginia

112. Letter to Mr. Henry Gannett, USGS, Washington D.C., from Francoise E. Matthes, Yosemite, California, dated Aug. 13, 1906.

113. Letter to Board on Geographic Names, from Otis Dock Marston, San Francisco, California, dated Sept. 15, 1976.

114. Letter to Mr. Tillotson, Superintendent of Grand Canyon National Park, Arizona from W. W. Bass, Wickenburg, Arizona, dated May 24, 1929.

115. Letter to Mr. Kilmartin, Executive Secretary BGN, Washington D.C. from P.T. Reilly, North Hollywood, California dated March 23, 1969.

116. Letter to Mr. Orth, Executive Secretary BGN, Washington, D.C. from P.T. Reilly, Sun City, Arizona dated May 23, 1986.

117. Letter to Mr. Kilmartin, Executive Secretary BGN, Washington, D.C. from P.T. Reilly, North Hollywood, California dated January 23, 1966.

118. Letter to Mr. Dingman, Executive Secretary, BGN, Washington, D.C. from P.T. Reilly, Sun City, Arizona dated October 4, 1974.

119. Letter to Hon. Henry M. Jackson, U.S. Senate, Washington, D.C. from Secretary of the Interior, dated April 22, 1969.

120. Letter to Frank Bond, Chairman BGN, Washington, D.C. from Superintendent Tillotson, Grand Canyon National Park, dated July 19, 1932.

Newspapers:

121. Arizona Enterprise. Sept. 19, 1891. The Grand Canyon: A Pen Picture of the Canyon by a Lady Visitor. By Virginia Dox, page 1.

122. Boston Transcript. July 8, 1929. Exit the Exotic Name. page 14.

123. Coconino Sun. Dec. 27, 1902. The Bright Angel: John Hance Tells Winfrield Hogaboom How That Place in the Grand Canyon Got Its Name. 19(52): 1.

124. Williams News. July 19, 1979. Park Ranger Accident Victim, Williams, Arizona.

Interpretive Brochures:

125. U.S Department of Interior. 1986. Glen Canyon Dam, Lake Powell. U.S. Government Printing Office, Washington, D.C.

126. Meadview Company. No date. Sportsman's Guide to Lake Mead. P.O. Box 247, Meadview, AZ 86444.

Other Information, Personal Communication, and Maps:

127. Information on file for Grand Canyon, Arizona, U.S. Board on Geographic Names, Reston, VA., and a computer printout (February 1992) of 498 records on 236 pg.

128. Jan Balsom, Archeologist, Grand Canyon National Park, Arizona

129. Barbara Brewer, Navajo Natural Heritage Program, Window Rock, Arizona

130. George Billinsgsley, U.S. Geological Survey, Flagstaff, Arizona

131. Harvey Butchart, Sun City, Arizona

132. Christopher Coder, National Park Service, Flagstaff, Arizona

133. Richard Quartaroli, Grand Canyon Book Search, Flagstaff, Arizona

134. John Rote, U.S.G.S., Water Resources Division, Flagstaff, Arizona

135. George Simmons, Euless, Texas

136. Peter Winn, Grand Junction, Colorado

137. Gene Buell, Tucson, Arizona

138. La Van Martineau, Globe, Arizona
139. Martin Litton, Menlo Park, California
140. Paul Martin, Phoenix, Arizona
141. Jim Mead, Flagstaff, Arizona
142. Bill Breed, Flagstaff, Arizona
143. Mike Ebersole, Grand Canyon, Arizona
144. Kim Crumbo, Grand Canyon, Arizona
145. Elston, D.P., G.H. Billingsley, R.A. Young (editors). 1989. Geology of Grand Canyon, Northern Arizona (with Colorado River Guides). Lee's Ferry to Pierce Ferry, Arizona, Field Trip Guidebook T115/315, American Geophysical Union, Washington, D.C., 239 pg.
146. Topographic Map of the Grand Canyon National Park, Arizona (West Half). Edition of 1927, Scale 1:48,000.
147. Ibid. (East Half).
148. Topographic Map of the Grand Canyon National Monument, Arizona. Edition of 1944, Reprinted 1961, Scale 1:48,000.
149. Topographic Map of Grand Canyon National Park and Vicity, Arizona. Edition of 1962, Scale 1:62,500.
150. Preliminary Geologic Map of the Grand Canyon and Vicinity, Arizona (Central and Western Sections). Edition of 1969, Scale 1:62,500.
151. Ibid. Eastern Section.
152. Jones, Leslie A. 1962. No Title. Roll map, Colorado River from Lee's Ferry to Pearce Ferry. Survey data from USGS 1923 Survey, Copyrighted 1960.
153. Glendening, Eber and Woody Shryock. 1979. Lees Ferry, Arizona. Grand Canyon Recreational Map Series, Map No. 1. Rainbow Exp., Tucson, map.
154. Briggs, Walter. 1976. Without Noise of Arms. Northland Press, Flagstaff, 212 pg.
155. Stegner, Wallace. 1953. Powell and the Names on the Plateau. The Western Humanities Review, Spring, Univ. of Utah, Salt Lake, pg 105-110.

"Grand Canon of the Colorado, Arizona," No. 4930, T.H. McAllister, Manufacturing Optician, 49 Nassau Street, New York.

168

INDEX

170

171

172

173

175

HELP TO PRESERVE THE GRAND CANYON!

The following non-profit organizations are working to preserve and protect the Grand Canyon. Contact them for more information on their activities, services, or how you can get involved.

GRAND CANYON NATURAL HISTORY ASSOCIATION: GCNHA is dedicated to assisting Grand Canyon National Park in interpretation and education. Their publishing program produces a wide range of pertinent and accurate information for park visitors in the areas of history, geology, botany, biology, trail guides, and maps. For information contact them at P.O. Box 399, Grand Canyon, AZ 86023, (602) 638-2481.

GRAND CANYON RIVER GUIDES: GCRG is a grassroots organization of professional river guides, private boaters, and general members founded in 1988. Its goals are protecting the resources of Grand Canyon, providing the highest quality river experience, and setting high standards for the river industry. GCRG is involved in issues involving the Grand Canyon, the Colorado River, and the community who have shared the river experience. For information or their newsletter, contact them at P.O. Box 1934, Flagstaff, AZ 86002.

GRAND CANYON TRUST: The GCT is a regional conservation organization dedicated to protecting, preserving, and managing wisely the public lands and diverse natural resources of the Colorado Plateau. Founded in 1985 and headquartered in Flagstaff, with an office in Washington, D.C., the GCT affects public policy through targeted scientific and economic research and analysis; public education, lobbying, cooperation with local communities, leaders, environmental organizations, and interest groups; and as a last resort, litigation. For information or their newsletter, contact them at Route 4, Box 718, Flagstaff, AZ 86001, (602) 774-7488.

INFORMATION ABOUT THIS BOOK

Some of the locations in *River to Rim* are cited as "origin unknown." When additional information becomes available, Earthquest Press plans to publish corrections and additions to this first edition. If you would like to receive this update, or if you have information on a place name listed or unlisted, please write to Earthquest Press, P.O. Box 1391, Flagstaff, AZ 86002-1391.

If you would like to obtain additional copies of *River to Rim*, please send $14.95 (plus shipping: $1.50 for one book and $.50 for each additional book) to Earthquest Press at the above address. Arizona residents please add the appropriate sales tax for your county. A check or money order must accompany your order. Bulk purchase inquiries invited.